TWILIGHT

FOR THE

WEST?

A CENTURY OF BLUNDERS AND APPEASEMENTS BY NAÏVE, NEOPHYTE POLITICIANS *1914-2014*

Richard Osborn

United States Air Force Veteran
British Army – Royal Artillery Veteran

RICHARD OSBORN

To my loving and devoted wife Barbara and family members who put up with me, while this book was being written.

Thank you for your patience.

_____

Twilight for the West? is a work of historical analysis, on the events of the last hundred years 1914 – 2014.

Cover *Baltic Sunset* photograph by: Richard Osborn

Britannia-American Books
ISBN: 9780692418413

BritanniaAmericanPublishing@yahoo.com

CONTENTS

THE AUTHOR

Richard Mervyn Osborn

He was born in 1937 in Wembley, England, less than a year after Edward VIII abdicated in favor of his brother King George VI. He was raised in England during and after the Second World War. He survived the German bombs by camping out at nights, in an air raid shelter, near Richmond Bridge and the River Thames. Richard went out into the garden after an air raid and picked up "chaff" (called window by the British and düppel by the Germans) that the Germans dropped to jam the radars.

TWILIGHT FOR THE WEST?

He was educated at Canterbury Cathedral Choir School and the King's School, Canterbury, where he listened extensively to the BBC radio and its accounts of post war Europe, including the Berlin airlift of 1948. He also became aware of the Dean of Canterbury Cathedral, Dr. Hewlett Johnson (also known as the Red Dean). It was a known fact that Dr. Johnson was an admirer of Mao Zedong and the Communist Chinese.

He is a veteran of the British Army and served in the Royal Artillery, during the Cyprus Emergency of the late 1950's. After emigrating from England to the United States in 1958, he served in the United States Air Force and worked on the Bomarc, a long range anti-aircraft missile. He is a graduate of California State University at Los Angeles in Marketing and of the Thunderbird Graduate School of International Management. He worked at General Dynamics on the Terrier/Tartar, Mauler and Standard missiles, Ford Aeronutronic, Hughes Aircraft and Tektronix. He is a licensed pilot and was the international marketing and sales manager for a Tektronix Inc. business unit.

Richard has travelled extensively around the world and visited the United Kingdom, France, Germany, Austria, The Netherlands, Belgium, Switzerland, Spain, Italy, Cyprus, Malta, Greece, Turkey, Norway Sweden, Finland, Poland, Estonia, Russia, Japan, Taiwan, Hong Kong, South Korea, The Philippines, Singapore, Malaysia, Indonesia, Thailand, India, Pakistan, South Africa, Brazil, Mexico and Canada.

Richard has always been a "student" of international affairs and the way nations have had

5

successes and failures in their international relations with other countries. He understood what appeasement was from an early age, since Neville Chamberlain (British Prime Minister) gave away Czechoslovakia to Hitler, in an attempt to persuade the German dictator not to absorb or attack other countries.

Now he is writing fiction and non-fiction in Knoxville, Tennessee. He has co-authored two novels to date: "Unbridled Power" and "On Her Majesty's Cyprus Mission".

PREFACE

The following saying has been attributed, by some people, to Sir Winston Churchill: "Those who fail to learn from history are doomed to repeat it."

Other people have attributed it to George Santayana, the Spanish/American philosopher, who originally said: "Those who cannot remember the past, are condemned to repeat it."

Whether Churchill paraphrased Santayana's original saying or not, it is immaterial. Churchill is correct that those who do not learn from history are going to make similar mistakes.

The twentieth century, which started out with great hope for the future, basically came to an end with the death of Queen Victoria in 1901. The last one hundred years has been full of blunders, mistakes, wars and appeasements. This book explores past issues that were critical in the development of the problems the *West* faces today.

Now in 2015, one century after the start of The Great War, the War to End All Wars or World War One, America and Europe are faced with major issues in the Middle East, Eastern Europe and the Far East. We must face these threats head on, or they will threaten the very freedoms and survival of this country. Unless our current leaders have learned from history, our future may not be too bright, as it has been for the past hundred years.

This book combines already known facts and history together, and it demonstrates how the West has helped develop its own geopolitical problems and issues. Whether one talks about World War Two, the Cold War, or the Middle East problems, the West has only itself and its naive leaders to blame, for all the strife during the last one hundred years.

The twilight (decline and fall) of the Roman Empire occurred over a fairly long period of time. The reasons should sound very familiar to the most readers of this book. The following is a partial list of the causes leading to the decline:

1. Discord between the Emperor and Senate
2. Decline in Morals and ethics
3. Weakening of the Legions, depending on mercenaries.
4. Government corruption and political volatility
5. Unemployment caused by immigrants (slaves)
6. Massive divide between the poor and the rich
7. Overspending by the Government
8. Towards the end, the games in the Coliseum used to placate the masses took up to one third of the Roman government budget
9. Economic problems and an economy that was failing

Carl von Clausewitz (1780-1831), who was a famous, Prussian, military thinker, developed theories on war and politics. There are many quotes attributed to him, and his ideas are taught at all military schools. Two of his better known quotes are:

1. *To secure peace is to prepare for war*
2. *Pursue one great decisive aim with force and determination.*

In addition, von Clausewitz studied past battles and campaigns, and concluded: we may infer that it is very difficult in the present state of Europe, for the most talented general to gain a victory over an enemy double his strength.

Napoleon Bonaparte has many quotes attributed to him, but one of the more important sayings for a Commander-in-chief is, "If you state you are going to take Vienna, TAKE VIENNA!" The meaning of this is that if you say you are going to do something, DO IT or don't say you are going to do it at all.

Sun Tzu (6th century BCE Chinese General) wrote many points about war and how to win. One issue he did emphasize was: "What is essential in war is **victory**, not prolonged operations." In other words, if you can muster overwhelming strength, go in quickly, win and get out.

Winston Churchill, 28th of May 1948, Perth, Scotland: "If you will not fight for the right when you can easily win without bloodshed; if you will not fight when your victory is sure and not too costly; you may come to the moment when you will have to fight with all the odds against you and only a precarious chance of survival. There may even be a worst case. You may have to fight when there is no hope of victory, because it is better to perish than to live as slaves."

Winston Churchill is quoted as saying, "An appeaser is one who feeds a crocodile – hoping it will eat him last."

Blunder Definition: A gross error or mistake resulting from ignorance or stupidity.

Appeasement Definition: When one nation yields or concedes to the belligerent demands of another nation in a conciliatory effort, at the expense of justice or other principles.

TWILIGHT FOR THE WEST?

This page intentionally left blank

1

World War One and Lenin
1914-1918

"Europe today is a powder keg and the leaders are like men smoking in an arsenal... A single spark will set off an explosion that will consume us all ... I cannot tell you when that explosion will occur, but I can tell you where ... *Some damned foolish thing in the Balkans will set it off.*" This was uttered by Otto von Bismarck, the German Chancellor, at the Congress of Berlin in 1878. Bismarck, often called the Iron Chancellor, was the chief architect of the German balance-of-power foreign policy that kept the peace in Europe for two decades, after the Franco–Prussian war ended in 1871.

The 28th of June 1914, was the start to events that would change the European political landscape and the world forever. Archduke Franz Ferdinand and Princess Sophie, his wife, went to visit Sarajevo in Bosnia-Herzegovina, a state which was part of the Austria-Hungary Empire. The purpose of the visit, by the heir to the throne, was to observe some military maneuvers in Bosnia. They were then scheduled to inspect a military barracks and to open a new state museum in Sarajevo.

TWILIGHT FOR THE WEST?

A gang of seventeen disgruntled Serbians made four attempts on the Archduke's life. The first two failed miserably, but the third one did kill about twenty people. However, it did not touch the intended target. Nonetheless, the third attempt set up the sequence of events that did lead to Archduke's assassination. On the way to the Sarajevo Town Hall for a reception, at 10:10 am, the convoy of six automobiles was hit by a grenade that was thrown by one of the Serbs, but it bounced off the Archduke's vehicle. It did kill several people in the next car, but not the Archduke. At 10:45 am, after the Town Hall reception, the Archduke decided to go to the Sarajevo hospital, where victims of the earlier attack were taken. This set up the events that led up to his assassination. The driver made a detour and just happened to approach where another assassin waited. As the Archduke's car came by, the assassin, Gavrilo Princip, shot both the heir to the throne and his wife. They both died shortly thereafter from their wounds.

There were rumors that the plotters were organized by the Serbian Military Intelligence. This prompted the Russians to promise Serbia that they would come to their aid, if there was any trouble with Austria. While all this was going on, French President Raymond Poincare and Prime Minister Rene Viviani left for a previously planned trip to Russia, on the 15th of July 1914. They were basically out of communications and contact with French military leaders, until they returned to Paris on the 29th of July 1914. Back in the early 1900's, radio communications from land to ship was in its infancy.

13

RICHARD OSBORN

Timeline of Events Leading Up to World War One

DATE	EVENTS
28 June 1914	Archduke Franz Ferdinand assassinated in Sarajevo by Serbians
15 July 1914	French President Poincare and PM Viviani left on trip to Russia
16 July 1914	British Foreign Minister "saw no urgency"
20 July 1914	French President Poincare and PM Viviani arrived in St. Petersburg
23 July 1914	French President Poincare and PM Viviani left Russia for France
23 July 1914	Austria-Hungary delivered 48 hour ultimatum to Serbia
25 July 1914	Austria-Hungary broke diplomatic relations with Serbia
28 July 1914	Austria-Hungary declared war on Serbia
28 July 1914	Russia mobilized troops in support of Serbia under treaty
28 July 1914	Germany mobilized troops in support of Austria-Hungary under treaty
29 July 1914	French President Poincare and PM Viviani arrived back in France
1 August 1914	Germany declared war on Russia
2 August 1914	France mobilizes troops under treaty with Russia
3 August 1914	Germany declared war on France
3 August 1914	France declared war on Germany
3 August 1914	France moved troops into Alsace and Lorraine
3 August 1914	Britain sent ultimatum to Germany based on 1839 Treaty with Belgium
4 August 1914	Britain declared war on Germany at 11:00 pm British time
28 October 1914	Turkey (Ottoman Empire) joined war on the side of Germany
4 November 1914	France, Britain, Russia declared war on Turkey
23 May 1915	Italy joined war on the side of France, Britain and Russia
6 April 1917	United States entered the war on the side of Britain and France
9 April 1917	Lenin traveled through Germany to Sweden on a train in a sealed compartment
11 November 1918	Armistice at 11:00 am ended the War to End all Wars

In the meantime, on the 23rd of July 1914, Austria-Hungary sent a list of demands to Serbia, known as the July Ultimatum. Serbia agreed to most of the demands, but that was not good enough for Austria-Hungary. On the 25th of July 1914, Austria-Hungary broke diplomatic relations with Serbia. Serbia received a telegram of support from Russia, and they mobilized their army.

The situation started to spin out of control, and three days later, on the 28th of July 1914, Austria-Hungary declared war on Serbia. The French diplomats were not due back in France until one day later. This date is considered the start of World War One, and it did not end until an armistice was declared, on the 11th of November 1918.

In response to Austria-Hungary declaration of war on Serbia, Russia mobilized its army and the "race" was on. Reacting to this, Germany then mobilized its forces. Based on all the alliances in force, the Central Powers, Germany and Austria-Hungary, faced off against France and Russia, called the Entente Powers. In a pact named the Treaty of London, signed in 1839 by Britain, France and Germany, the neutrality of Belgium was guaranteed. For seventy-five years, up until 1914, this treaty was honored and was not violated.

Then, at the beginning of August 1914, Germany accused France of planning to attack Germany through Belgium and, if they did not stop their provocations, Germany would attack France through Belgium. However, Belgium would not give Germany permission to transport its troops through their country which left Germany no alternative, but to invade the country. Based on the Treaty of London, Britain had no choice, but to declare war on Germany, after the Germans attacked neutral Belgium, Holland and Luxembourg. The Germans attacked these three neutral countries, as part of the Schlieffen Plan for victory. Count Alfred Graf von Schlieffen formulated a plan that required Germany to defeat France in eight weeks, like they did in the 1870 Franco-Prussian war. Then the Germans could place the full weight of their troops against Russia. They were afraid of a war on two fronts. This attack on the neutral powers was a major **BLUNDER,** since it gave Britain a reason to join the fray. British troops, together with Commonwealth forces, greatly altered the balance-of-power on the Western Front. The entire military situation changed for Germany, with Britain entering the war, and Schlieffen's plan could not easily be achieved. Now Germany had a major war on two fronts.

All the combatants thought that they would win a quick war, and the troops would be home by Christmas. There was a nationalistic fervor in all countries, and most citizens thought it would be a short war, which would not affect them very much.

By 1917, Germany decided that the war was not going well, and they needed to somehow get Russia out of the hostilities. They could then concentrate their forces on the Western Front. How were they to do that? The German government came up with the idea of helping Vladimir Lenin to travel from Switzerland, where he was in self-exile for safety reasons, to Sweden from where he could easily get back to Russia. Since Europe was in the throes of a major war, Lenin needed to cross Germany, in order to reach Sweden.

On the 9th of April 1917, Lenin and twenty nine fellow Russian exiles in Bern, Switzerland boarded a train for Zurich. From there, they travelled to Gottmadingen which was just over the border inside Germany. They then drove from Gottmadingen to Singen, where they boarded a train provided by Germany.

Vladimir Lenin

Lenin and his supporters were installed in a sealed carriage that was hauled by the German train to Frankfurt, then Berlin and finally ended up in Sassnitz, on the 12th of April. Lenin then embarked on the Sassnitz-Trelleborg ferry and arrived in Sweden on the 13th of April. From here he went by train from Stockholm to Petrograd (St. Petersburg), which was then part of the Finnish Province of Russia. He arrived at Petrogad on the 16th of April 1917, just before midnight.

For the next few months, Russia was in chaos, but on the 26th of October 1917, at last the Soviets achieved their objective and took over the government, with Lenin as chairman. After a lot of discussion and bickering among the communist leaders, Russia ultimately withdrew from World War One, on the 3rd of March, 1918. The Germans had achieved their objective and could now concentrate their forces on the Western Front.

Note: Some dates may appear incorrect in this history of Russia. Up until 1918, Russia used the Julian calendar while the rest of the West used the Gregorian calendar. In 1918, Russia switched to the Gregorian calendar except for the Russian Orthodox Church, which still uses the Julian.

Situation Analysis:

The German agreement to allow Lenin to travel through Germany to Sweden, on the surface, appeared to be a good one. The objective was to get Russia out of the War, and thus allow Germany to move forces to the Western Front. In the end, this did not help Germany win the war. In fact, in November 1918, they sued for peace, and an armistice was agreed to. Under terms of the armistice, fighting ceased at 11:00 am on the 11th day of the 11th month.

Allowing Lenin to travel through Germany, and thus reach Russia, would have unforeseen consequences for the next seventy years, around the world. According to all records, Kaiser Wilhelm ll, the Emperor of Germany, until he abdicated on the 9th of November 1918, knew nothing about the agreement to let Lenin travel through Germany. In fact, the German Chancellor, Theobald von Bethmann-Hollweg, made the decision on his own volition and did not even mention it to Kaiser Wilhelm ll.

German Chancellor
Theobald von
Bethman-Hollweg

Germany committed two major **BLUNDERS** during the war. The first one was the decision to attack Belgium, under the Schlieffen plan, which resulted in Great Britain joining the war on France's side. The second blunder was allowing Lenin to travel through the country, so he could get back to Russia and create a revolution.

Of course, one could argue the biggest mistake, the Germans made, was to start the war to begin with. However, under a treaty with Austria-Hungary, Germany was committed to come to their support if they were attacked. The assassination of Archduke Ferdinand set off a sequence of events that no one could stop. Europe was divided into two major camps by treaty – the Central Powers (Germany and Austria/Hungary) and the Entente Powers (France and Russia). Great Britain was not in either of the power blocs, but was a signatory to the Treaty of London, guaranteeing the neutrality of Belgium. The Great War started with both sides claiming they would be victorious, and it would be over by Christmas 1914.

However, the war lasted four years, with over eight million soldiers being killed on both sides and twenty one million soldiers being wounded. It ended up into trench warfare that had never before been seen, and neither side achieved victory. When the US entered the war in 1917, the Germans slowly became outnumbered and had to sue for peace.

2

League of Nations
1919-1946

Officially, the League of Nations lasted exactly twenty-six years and three months, but in actuality it only lasted, at the most, eleven years. The League was founded on the 10th of January 1920, a little over a year after the Great War came to a conclusion, with the armistice of 1918. The idea of an international organization, to prevent war, first gathered support in 1914, mainly in Great Britain and the United States. Lord Bryce, of Great Britain, helped found a group of pacifists that became known as the Bryce Group. A similar group in the United States was formed in 1915 and included many politicians, including William Howard Taft.

When the Great War ended with the armistice, a Paris Peace Conference commenced on the 18th of January 1919, attended by the four great allied powers (the Big Four); France, Britain, Italy, United States. Six months later, on the 28th of June 1919, the war with Germany officially ended, when they together with the allied powers (except the US) and signed the Treaty of Versailles. Other treaties were signed later in 1919 and 1920 with Hungary, Austria, Bulgaria and Turkey (Ottoman Empire). Out of the Paris Peace

Conference came the foundation of the League of Nations, but the United States never ratified the Treaty of Versailles or the League of Nations, because the US Senate couldn't muster the necessary votes to approve it. However, on the 25th of August 1921, the Treaty of Berlin was signed, between the US and Germany, officially ending the war between the two countries.

Part 1 of the Treaty of Versailles established the League but, with the US Senate not approving the treaty, the League never became the organization envisioned by the founders. The US withdrew into a form of neutralism that would last until the attack by Japan at Pearl Harbor. The League attempted to bring about major disarmament by all powers, but it floundered on the fear, by some countries, that they would be attacked by Germany, if they disarmed.

There was an initial agreement by France, Great Britain, Italy and Japan that they would limit the size of their navies, but this ultimately ended in failure. The League seemed to work in preventing war fairly effectively, for the first eleven years.

Out of the Treaty of Versailles and the founding of the League, some major decisions were made that would have consequences for years to come. First, Germany was stripped of territory, such as the SAAR, Rhineland, Danzig area, and the Sudetenland. In addition, Germany's African colonies were divided among the British, French and other countries. Second, new countries were formed out of the old Empires and given independence, such as Austria, Hungary, Poland, Yugoslavia, Syria, Iraq, Latvia, etc.

TWILIGHT FOR THE WEST?

Formation and Results of the League of Nations

DATES	EVENTS
11 November 1918	World War I ended with armistice, took place at 11:00 am on the 11th November 1918
18 January 1919	Paris Peace Conference commenced with the Big Four Britain, France, Italy and the U.S.
28 June 1919	World War I officially ended with the signing of the Treaty of Versailles
10 January 1920	League of Nations founded as a result of the Paris Peace Conference
19 March 1920	U.S. President Woodrow Wilson failed to win the League Senate approval by 7 votes
25 August 1921	The Treaty of Berlin officially ended the war between Germany and the United States
19 September 1931	Japan invaded Manchuria and set up puppet regime
30 January 1933	Adolf Hitler became German Chancellor and started rearmament against League rules
24 February 1933	Japan announced it was leaving the League of Nations over its Manchuria vote
14 October 1933	Germany left the League of Nations because it wanted to rearm
1 March 1935	The SAAR land was officially integrated into Germany and the German army entered it.
3 October 1935	Italy invaded Abyssinia and Emperor Haile Selassie appealed to the League to no avail
7 March 1936	Germany remilitarized the Rhineland forbidden under the Treaty of Versailles
17 July 1936	The Spanish Civil War commenced with Germany and Russians testing equipment
13 December 1937	Italy left the League of Nations after censure over its Abyssinia invasion
7 July 1937	Japan launched a full scale invasion of China having already taken Manchuria
1 September 1939	World War II started with the German and Russian attack on Poland
14 August 1945	World War II ended with the unconditional surrender of Japan
12 April 1946	Final meeting of the League of Nations to discuss the use of assets
20 April 1946	United Nations replaced the League of Nations and obtained all the assets

The League inherited the former Middle East territories of the Ottoman Empire, with France and Great Britain being given mandate power to run them. Bureaucrats from these two countries got together and drew lines on the map, which carved out new countries in the Middle East. This process did not take into account the different tribes or religious factions. Sunnis, Shiites and Kurds were placed in the same country, with total disregard on how the country would be organized or governed.

The first country to withdraw from the League was Costa Rica on the 22nd of January 1925, just five years after joining the organization. The next country to leave the League was Brazil on the 14th of June 1926. Over the next thirteen years, many countries left the League, because they either saw no value in being members or they disagreed with the decisions being made. The last country to leave the organization was the Soviet Union, although it was actually expelled for invading Finland in 1939.

The 1930's saw major problems cropping up for the League of Nations, and these issues reduced it to a bloviating organization (debating society). The League became ineffective in preventing one country invading another, or in stopping countries from breaking the basic articles and treaties of the organization.

The first major power to leave the League was Japan, on the 24th of February 1933, over the League's vote to sanction Japan, due to its invasion of Manchuria. On the 18th of September 1931, the Japanese military invaded Manchuria, after staging a false flag operation on the South Manchurian Railway, near Mukden. The Japanese placed a bomb near the tracks and blamed it on China. Using this as an excuse, the Japanese military invaded Manchuria on the 19th of September 1931 and obtained victory by the 8th of February 1932. Inner Manchuria, as it was known, was declared an independent state by Japan. In actuality, Japan ran it, so they could obtain the raw resources, desperately needed by their country.

Adolf Hitler became Chancellor of Germany in early 1933 and, by the fall of 1933, he decided that membership in the League was of no value to Germany. On the 14th of October 1933, Germany withdrew from the League, because it wanted to rearm, which was forbidden by the Treaty of Versailles and the League of Nations. The major powers in the League did nothing about this, and it was the first step in the appeasement of Germany by Britain and France.

Under terms of the Treaty of Versailles and the League of Nations, the SAAR land (part of Germany) was administered by France, under a fifteen year mandate. Its major resource was coal that was used by Germany to assist in the creation of steel. In addition, it also contained many factories and railway centers. In early 1935, this fifteen year mandate ran out and, on the 13th of January 1935, a plebiscite (vote) was held in the SAAR, to determine which nation the people wanted to be part of. Ninety-eight percent of the population voted to rejoin the German Reich. Seven weeks after this plebiscite, the SAAR did rejoin Germany, and a German commissioner was placed in charge, by Hitler. This event, allowed by the League, encouraged Hitler to take further steps in bringing back into the Reich, lands stripped away by the Treaty of Versailles.

In October 1935, Italy invaded Ethiopia in the second Italian Abyssinian War, which was in direct violation of Article X of the League of Nations. Article X stated that League members were obligated to aid any member attacked or invaded, by a foreign power. Italy was a member of the League, and it invaded another League member in clear violation of the Article. The war ended in May 1936 with Italy occupying Ethiopia. The League did nothing about this invasion, and this further reduced the effectiveness of the League. Under the cover of this war, Hitler remilitarized the Rhineland, on the 7th of March 1936, clearly in violation of the League. Britain and France did nothing, because they were preoccupied with the Italian-Ethiopian war. This occupation of the Rhineland was a gamble on Hitler's part, and he was opposed by the military, for taking such a risk. From then on, the German military was under the "heel" of Hitler. Hitler was quoted as saying "The forty-eight hours after the march into the Rhineland were the most nerve-racking of my life. If the French had then marched into the Rhineland, we would have had to withdraw with our tails between our legs."

From here on, the League of Nations became irrelevant and it was unable to stop any aggression. In 1937, Germany tested its new Air Force (Luftwaffe) in the Spanish Civil War, which would become a testing ground of Germany's World War Two airplanes. Italy departed from the League on the 13th of December 1937 due to its censure by the organization over its invasion of Ethiopia. The Soviet Union was expelled from the League on the 30th of November 1939, because it invaded Finland. Why it was never expelled for its invasion of Poland, on the 17th of September 1939, has never been explained? Under the German Russian Non-aggression Pact signed in August 1939, Stalin was given the eastern part of Poland and the three small Baltic States of Estonia, Latvia and Lithuania. The invasion of these states has also never been explained by the League.

At the end of World War Two, the United Nations was formed, and any assets, belonging to the League of Nations, were transferred to the UN. The final meeting of the League took place on the 12th of April 1946, and the UN took over all assets on the 26th of April 1946.

Situation Analysis:

The League of Nations was formed under the idealistic thinking of Lord Bryce and others. Even Woodrow Wilson got into the act, but then he could not get the votes, to insure passage in the US Senate. Even, if the US had joined the League, it is doubtful that the effectiveness of the organization would have been much different. The main European victors, France, Italy and Great Britain, in the Great War wanted retribution and they wanted Germany to pay for the war, even though they didn't start it. Austria-Hungary actually started it, by attacking Serbia. Regardless, Germany was forced to pay, and this left Germany bankrupt. It became open to any demigod that came along. Adolf Hitler and the Nazis filled this desire for revenge, on the part of the Germans. This was a major **BLUNDER** on the part of the Big Four, the Treaty of Versailles and the League of Nations

The League of Nations survived the first ten years intact, except for a few minor countries dropping out. After that, it was a slide downhill, until World War Two commenced. Initially the League did some good by resolving some minor disputes between nations and creating new nations from the old empires. However, two major factors got in the way of real effectiveness. They were the depression that started in October, 1929, and nationalism that had always been around.

The League was really in trouble, when Japan, one of the four great nations and a Council member, decided to invade Manchuria. The Asian country was heavily censured and it left the League in 1931. The League did nothing about their attack on China and this was another major **BLUNDER**. Two European countries, Germany and Italy, closely watched the reaction of the League to the Japanese invasion of China, and they decided that the lack of response by the League members indicated the organization was impotent.

The **APPEASEMENT** by Britain and France, when Germany entered the Rhineland and started remilitarizing, further reduced the effectiveness of the League. In 1937, the two major powers further appeased another country, Italy, after it invaded and took over Abyssinia. Sanctions were placed on Italy, but after it conquered Ethiopia, Britain decided that the sanctions were not working and lifted them. Hitler watched all this and decided that Britain and France would do about anything, to avoid another war.

The League of Nations was dreamed up by pacifists and intellectual liberals; it was not based on reality. They did not consider nationalism and human nature. Unfortunately, many of today's politicians have not studied or learned from history, and they believe that all you have to do is treat your enemies nicely, and they will be nice to you. Unfortunately, history has proven otherwise.

3

Germany and Great Britain – 1930s Appeasement

Great Britain came out of World War One with the idea that it was the war to end all wars. They suffered 702,917 deaths and 1,663,570 wounded, in just four years. They did not want to go to war again. Almost a whole generation of young people was affected by the hostilities. The politicians of the day wanted someone to pay for all the cost and suffering. The easiest target was Germany and, under the Treaty of Versailles, they were required to pay huge sums to the victors.

However, by the 1930s, the British Government felt that the Germans had been penalized too severely, and it started to sympathize with the Germans plight. After the Japanese invasion of China, the Italian war in Ethiopia and the German takeover of the SAAR land, Britain started to negotiate with the Hitler government, about the strict naval terms of the Versailles Treaty on Germany. The British, under Prime Minister Ramsey MacDonald and then Prime Minister Stanley Baldwin, negotiated a new agreement with Hitler, about the size of the German navy.

The British were obsessed with the thought that the Germans would attack Britain in the future with bombers, and they thought that by allowing the Germans some naval forces, this would appease Hitler and his military. They thought that they could control the German navy, no matter how large it became. In May 1935, the British entered into serious negotiations with the Germans, about the size and makeup of their naval forces (Kreigsmarine). Hitler had made some speeches in which he disavowed any race in naval forces, akin to what happened before 1914. Hitler recognized Britain's requirement for a large navy to protect its empire.

Based on his "peaceful" oration, the British agreed to a ratio of 35:100 in naval forces. In other words, the Germans were to be allowed to grow their tonnage to 35% of the Royal Navy tonnage. The negotiations were carried on between Britain and Germany, without the approval of the other two major countries in the League of Nations; namely Italy and France.

Finally, on the 18th of June 1935, the Anglo-German Naval Agreement was signed by both sides and, on the 12th of July 1935, the agreement was registered with the League of Nations. As mentioned in the previous chapter, the League by this time was already ineffective, and there was little protest by the organization, over this bilateral agreement between Britain and Germany. The British went home believing they had Hitler under control, while the German dictator came to realize that the British would do almost anything, to avoid another war like the First World War.

Timeline of Events Leading Up to World War Two

DATES	EVENTS
10 January 1920	The Treaty of Versailles was signed and the SAAR land controlled by Britain and France
30 January 1933	Adolf Hitler became Chancellor of Germany and started plotting how to grab power
27 February 1933	The Reichstag was burned and Hitler used it as an excuse to nullify civil liberties
13 January 1935	After the 15 year agreement was over, a plebiscite was held, Saar joined Germany
1 March 1935	The SAAR land was officially integrated into Germany and the German army entered it.
18 June 1935	Anglo-German Naval Agreement changed the limits on the size of German Kriegsmarine
7 March 1936	Germany remilitarized the Rhineland forbidden under the Treaty of Versailles
28 May 1936	Neville Chamberlain became Prime Minister of Britain after Stanley Baldwin resigned
10 December 1936	King Edward VII abdicated in favor of his younger brother King George VI
27 April 1937	German Air Force tested their aircraft in Spanish civil war attack on Guernica
12 March 1938	The Anschluss incorporated Austria into Germany without any fighting
15 September 1938	Chamberlain flew to meet with Adolf Hitler at Berchtesgaden to discuss Sudetenland
22 September 1938	Chamberlain flew to meet Adolf Hitler at Godesberg to further discuss Sudetenland
29 September 1938	Chamberlain left Britain for the third and final meeting with Adolf Hitler at Munich
30 September 1938	Chamberlain returned to England waving the "famous" paper PEACE IN OUR TIME
15 March 1939	Germany took over the rest of Czechoslovakia without a fight.
31 August 1939	Germans dressed as Poles invaded German radio station in the Gleiwitz incident
1 September 1939	Nazi Germany invaded Poland after staging a false flag operation against a radio station
3 September 1939	England and France declared war on Germany under treaty with Poland
10 May 1940	Neville Chamberlain resigned and Winston Churchill became Prime Minster

The Germans believed the Naval Agreement was the start of an Anglo-German alliance, against France and the Soviet Union. The British, however, believed it was the start of arms limitations on the Germans, which would limit their expansionism aims. The British pacifists and appeasers of the day believed that they could control Hitler, and maybe even force him out of office.

When the German troops marched into the Rhineland in 1936, Hitler gambled that the British and French would not present a problem, since they did not want to start another war in Europe, so soon after the last horrific struggle in Belgium and France. Hitler was proved correct, and he took aim at his next targets; Austria and Czechoslovakia.

In late 1937 and early 1938, Germany pushed for the union of Austria with Germany. The Germans claimed that most Austrians spoke German and were therefore really Germans. Hitler wanted Austria to become part of Germany, just as the Rhineland had been absorbed in 1936. This was, however, forbidden under the Treaty of Versailles. Hitler decided the only way, to bring Austria into Germany, was to destabilize the country.

Starting in 1934, Hitler ordered the Austrian Nazis to create problems for the Austrian Government, under Chancellor Dollfuss. By 1936, a new Austrian Chancellor, by the name of Schuschnigg, tried to keep Austria independent, by negotiating with Hitler. They signed the German Austrian agreement, which recognized the independence of Austria. Schuschnigg believed this agreement was enough to appease the

German dictator. In the same year, Germany and Italy agreed to become allies in a Rome-Berlin axis. This took away any support Austria could count on from Italy.

On the 9th of March 1938, Schuschnigg announced that he planned to hold a referendum, in which the Austrians could vote whether they wanted to be part of Germany. Hitler was against this, since it could go against Germany and remove any pretext for invading Austria. Hitler persuaded Schuschnigg to call it off. Schuschnigg did and he immediately resigned thereafter. The new Austrian Chancellor, Arthur Seyss-Inquart, asked Germany for help in restoring order and, on the 12th of March 1938, German troops marched into Austria unopposed. The event was known as the Anschluss (Union).

A month later, Hitler held his own referendum and the result was not in question, as in any dictatorship. The overwhelming majority voted to be part of Germany. Another nail had been hammered into the coffin of the League of Nations. Hitler now had most of the German speaking people part of Germany; that was except the Sudetenland. The Sudetenland was a border area of Czechoslovakia, located on the frontier with Germany.

The country of Czechoslovakia was created out of the Austria-Hungary Empire that collapsed at the end of World War One. The Versailles Treaty and the League of Nations guaranteed the independence of this new country, and it was made up of four regions; Bohemia, Moravia-Silesia, Slovakia and Sub-Carpathian Rus. Seventy years later, on the 1st of

January 1993, Bohemia/Moravia-Silesia would be known as the Czech Republic and Slovakia/Sub-Carpathian Rus became Slovakia; two independent countries.

Hitler had eyes on Czechoslovakia ever since he took office and dreamed of a greater Germany. The former Kingdom of Bohemia, now part of Czechoslovakia, contained many German speaking nationals; mainly in the Sudetenland. Hitler, having now gobbled up Austria, set his sights on the Sudetenland and Czechoslovakia.

On the 28th of March 1938, Konrad Henlein, head of the Sudetenland Nazi party, met with Hitler, where he was ordered to foment as much trouble as possible. Hitler gambled that Britain and France would not go to war over Czechoslovakia. However, just in case, he made plans (Operation Green) to invade the country.

Neville Chamberlain travelled to Germany three times in September 1938, in order to find a resolution to the crisis created by Hitler and Henlein. Britain wanted to avoid war under all circumstances.

On the 15th of September 1938, Chamberlain traveled to Berchtesgaden and met with Hitler in his mountain retreat. In the three hour meeting, Hitler told Chamberlain that, if he was willing to accept self-determination for the Germans in Sudetenland, the German government was willing to discuss the issue. Chamberlain flew back to England and held a meeting with his cabinet.

While these discussions were going on between Hitler and Chamberlain, Hans Oster, a German general, was planning a coup to remove Hitler from power. This never went very far, because during the next two weeks, Chamberlain appeased Hitler, and the dictator won without war.

One week later, on the 22nd of September, Chamberlain flew back to Germany and met Hitler at Godesberg. At this meeting, Hitler upped the ante and told Chamberlain, since Czechoslovakia was making life unbearable for Germans, he wanted the country dissolved. Chamberlain was shaken up by these new demands.

Finally, at the third meeting in Munich, on the 29th of September 1938, Chamberlain of Britain, Daladier of France, Mussolini of Italy and Hitler signed the Munich agreement.   This gave the Sudetenland to Germany, and in return German promised to allow the rest of Czechoslovakia to remain free.   Chamberlain returned to Britain, waving the piece of paper in his hand, declaring "Peace In Our Time".

Chamberlain, Daladier, Hitler and Mussolini at the Munich Conference

This appeasement by Chamberlain would dog him for the rest of his life. Hitler tore up the piece of paper, and six months later, on the 15th of March 1939, German troops marched into the rest of

Czechoslovakia and took it over, without a shot being fired. Hitler was now ready to take on his next target (Poland) that he thought he could obtain, without getting into a war with Great Britain or France. If he couldn't get it without a fight, he believed that the German troops would win in a war anyway.

Situation Analysis:

Britain was one of the "big four" and was a signatory of the Treaty of Versailles and the League of Nations. However, in the 1920s and 1930s, pacifists were everywhere in England, mainly because of the slaughter of World War One. Starting with the invasion of China by the Japanese and continuing with the takeover of parts of Ethiopia by the Italians, Britain acquiesced and started to conduct its own affairs, without consultation with the other major powers.

Starting in 1935, the British, under Prime Minister MacDonald and then Baldwin, negotiated a naval agreement with the Nazi government, without consulting France, Italy or the United States. The British thought they could contain Hitler by appeasing him. Neville Chamberlain continued this appeasement at Munich over the Sudetenland and Czechoslovakia. Some argue that Chamberlain gave in to Hitler, in order to give Britain time to build up its forces. This can hardly be true since at every turn, Winston Churchill was labeled as a war monger, when he warned about Nazi Germany.

The **APPEASEMENT** of the dictator Hitler is cited in most history books and documents that cover that era. Chamberlain and the pacifists of the 1930s really believed that if one is nice to a dictator, they will be nice to you. In fact, one still sees this reasoning today, when the West is negotiating with Iran or Russia.

There were some people at the Munich meeting that overheard Hitler shouting because Chamberlain had given in. Hitler had plans to march into the Sudetenland, even if Chamberlain did not accede to his demands. When Chamberlain returned to England after signing the Munich agreement, he firmly believed he had saved his country from war. He trusted Hitler to adhere to his promise that he did not want any more territory in Europe.

Hitler, on the other hand, was asked by Goering why he had signed the agreement, giving up any more territorial demands. Hitler replied that "It is just a piece of paper". Six months later, Hitler tore up this piece of paper and took over the rest of Czechoslovakia; so much for Chamberlain's **APPEASEMENT**. Six more months after this, Hitler invaded Poland and World War Two commenced.

World War Two could have been prevented, if the League of Nations and its major powers had not appeased Hitler. This war resulted in twenty-two million to twenty-five million military deaths and many millions of civilian deaths. Neville Chamberlain, by giving in at Munich, caused the deaths of three hundred and eighty three thousand British military members. Chamberlain's **APPEASEMENT**, at Munich, is still discussed today, and it is given out, as a case study, in university history classes, on how not to negotiate with dictators or potential enemies.

4

The China Problem

On the 12th of February 1912, the last Emperor of China abdicated, and China became a republic with a president. For the next few years, there was considerable instability in China until, in 1919, Sun Yat-sen became the Premier of China. Under his guidance, the following years in China were fairly peaceful. During this time, in 1921, the Chinese Communist Party (CCP) was formed under the guidance of Comintern representatives from the Soviet Union.

On the 12th of March 1925, Sun Yat-sen died of cancer and Chiang Kai-shek took over as leader of the Chinese Nationalist Party or Kuomintang (KMT), as it was known. However, China was not unified, as the Communists and minor war lords continuously created problems. Initially, Chiang had support from the Soviets, because Stalin was concerned that the Chinese Communists might be competitive with the Soviet Union.

In 1926-1927, the peasants of Hunan Province were organized by the Communists, under Mao

Zedong. Later in 1927, Chiang had many of the Chinese labor leaders and the Communists killed, since they opposed the KMT. By 1928, most of China was under the control of the KMT, and the capital was moved to Nanjing. The country enjoyed some fairly peaceful years, and the economy began to grow. However, this quiet period did not last very long.

In November 1931, the Chinese Soviet Republic was created and named Mao Zedong, as its chairman. The capital was located in Jiangxi. For the next two to three years, Chiang began a campaign to wipe out the Communists, as he saw them as a threat to his power.

In 1934, Chiang planned an attack on the CCPs capital, but the Communists heard of the plan and began the LONG March from Jiangxi to Shaanxi. During this eight thousand mile march, they lost up to ninety percent of their supporters.

Soon, the KMT and the CCP put aside the civil war and made an uneasy peace, so they could fight the Japanese who had invaded Manchuria and were now invading other parts of China.

The United States allowed volunteers to go and support the Chinese, in their fight against Japan. The AVG (American Volunteer Group) under Chennault attacked Japanese planes, using Curtiss P-40s. The group was very successful, and they were called "The Flying Tigers". The United States, after the attack on Pearl Harbor, on the 7th of December, started to support the Chinese openly, with arms and money. This aid allowed the Chinese to increase their war fighting effort against the Japanese.

Timeline of Events Leading Up to Communist China

DATES	EVENTS
12 February 1912	Abdication of Puyi, the last emperor of the Qing dynasty.
10 March 1912	Yuan Shikai became president of China and period of unrest began until 1919
10 October 1919	Sun Yat-sen became premier of the Republic of China
12 March 1925	Sun Yat-sen died of liver cancer at the Peking College Hospital
12 April 1928	Chiang Kai-shek leader of Kuomintang had a purge of the communists in China
16 October 1934	To avoid being captured, the communists began their LONG march from Jiangxi
22 October 1935	The Communists LONG march evading Chiang Kai-shek ended in Shaanxi Province
7 July 1937	Second Sino-Japanese War began with Japan forces fighting at Lugou bridge
13 December 1937	Nanking fell to the Japanese and the rape of Nanking began (Nanking massacre)
6 October 1939	The Chinese won a victory at Changsha and a stalemate period in the war began
9 September 1945	Japanese troops in China surrendered and the eight year occupation ended
26 June 1946	Full scale war broke out between the Communists and the Nationalists
30 June 1947	The Communists crossed the Huanghe (Yellow) River, entered the Dabie Mountains
24 September 1948	The Communists captured Jinan and Shendong province
20 November 1948	The Battle of Pingjin began with Communists fighting for control of China's capital
31 January 1949	The capital city of Beijing (Peiping, Peking) fell to the Communists
23 April 1949	The Communists captured the Kuomintang capital of Nanjing
1 October 1949	Mao Zedong declared establishment of the PRC (Peoples Republic of China)
1 March 1950	Chiang Kai-shek resumed his presidency of the Republic of China on Taiwan (Formosa)
25 November 1950	Chinese offensive took place across the Yalu river driving the UN forces back in Korea

From 1941 until August 1945, the Chinese put aside their civil war and focused on fighting the invading Japanese. In August 1945, two events happened that would change the entire situation in China. First, the Soviets entered the war against Japan by invading Manchuria, and they drove the Japanese troops back. Second, the atomic bomb attacks on Hiroshima and Nagasaki abruptly ended the war. Many of the surrendering Japanese troops gave their weapons to the Chinese Communists or the Soviet forces. The Communists were then able to use these weapons against the Nationalists.

Late in the middle of 1946, the Chinese civil war started up again, with the Kuomintang, under Chiang Kai-shek, fighting the Communists led by Mao Zedong and supported by the Soviets. Even though Stalin was suspicious of Mao, he still supported him, with the goal of expanding the communist philosophy and empire.

The Truman administration was focused on the Soviet threat in Europe, and it did not analyze the threat a Communist takeover in China would have on the rest of Asia. In December 1945, President Truman finally sent George C Marshall, as a special envoy to China, to try and negotiate a settlement between the two sides. The Truman administration had little idea that Mao wanted to take over China and had no intention of seriously negotiating an agreement. It was just like Neville Chamberlain and Adolf Hitler in 1938 at Munich. General Marshall's visit was almost a waste of time, as many bureaucrats in the U.S. State Department sympathized with the so called agrarian reformers, led by Mao Zedong. They were all naïve, and by February 1947, the Marshall mission was a failure and he returned to the U.S.

Zhang Qun, George C. Marshall and Zhou Enlai trying to negotiate an end to the civil war

A truce was called while the negotiations continued, but when General Marshall departed China for home, the combatants continued the civil war. At this point, the United States concentrated on building up Western Europe, under the Marshall plan, and basically the Nationalists were "thrown under the bus", by the Truman administration.

By June 1947, the Communists crossed the Yellow River and entered the Dabie Mountains. A year later, in September 1948, the Communists captured the province of Shedong and the capital city of Jinan. This capture was facilitated by the defection of the KMT general in the region, along with eight thousand troops.

In November 1948, the Battle of Pingjin commenced, and it would decide the fate of China. After fierce fighting, the Communists finally took the Chinese capital of Beijing (Peiping, Peking) on the 31st of January 1949. Three months later, on the 23rd of April 1949, the Communists captured the Nationalist capital of Nanjing. For all intents and purposes, the battle for China was over, and the Nationalists fled to Taiwan (Formosa).

On the 1st of October 1949, Mao Zedong declared the foundation of the Peoples Republic of China (PRC) and, on the 1st of March 1950, Chiang Kai-shek resumed the Presidency of the Republic of China on Taiwan (Formosa). The PRC has always claimed that Taiwan is part of China, and it has threatened to invade the island many times, since 1950.

In October 1949, the Soviet Union officially recognized the PRC as the legitimate government of China. In December of the same year, Mao Zedong went to Moscow to consult with Joseph Stalin, and while there, he signed a treaty of alliance with the Soviet Union. He also began initial discussions about a possible invasion of South Korea by the North. Stalin, at this time, was not in favor of this action, but he changed his opinion a year later.

Mao Zedong, Joseph Stalin and East German leader Walter Ulbricht

For the next thirty years, the Communists, under Mao Zedong, ran China and changed the society in several ways. The first eight years saw the Communists extending control over the entire country. From 1958 to 1961, Mao wanted to transform the country from an agrarian to a pure communist society. This was known as the Great Leap Forward and resulted in a great famine. This famine caused the deaths of an estimated eighteen to forty-five million people. The result was that Mao lost some influence in the Party.

Then in 1966 to 1976, Mao Zedong started the Cultural Revolution that saw persecutions, harassment and property seizure of millions of Chinese. Finally, after Mao died in 1976, a new, more realistic Deng Xiaoping took over, and China started to grow economically. However, even today, the Party still does not allow any deviation from its communist philosophy.

For many years, after the Communist takeover in 1949, the United States still recognized the Republic of China (ROC) on Taiwan, as the legitimate government of China. It was a permanent member of the United Nations Security Council. However in 1971, after much debate by the Western Powers, the United States, under President Nixon, agreed to the transfer of the permanent seat on the Security Council to the PRC delegate. The US is still pledged to the defense of Taiwan, should it be attacked. Whether the US would actually go to war with the PRC over Taiwan is still an open question.

Situation Analysis:

The Truman Administration's handling of the China issue, after World War Two, was nothing short of a major **BLUNDER**. Yes, there was corruption within the Nationalist government but, with the influence the US government had on the KMT, Chiang Kai-shek could have been persuaded to make changes. Regardless, a Communist government in China was obviously ten times worse than a non perfect KMT government. Truman "threw the KMT under the bus", based on bad information from George C Marshall (Secretary of State 1947-1949), Dean Acheson and others in his administration.

American President Harry S. Truman 1945-1952

Dean Acheson, the Secretary of State from 1949 – 1953, ran the State Department, and one of his associates was a man, by the name of Alger Hiss. Hiss had been accused of being a communist spy, by a former member of the American communist party, Whittaker Chambers. Although the statute of limitations had run out on any spying charges, Hiss was found guilty on two counts of perjury and sentenced to two consecutive, five year terms in jail. Dean Acheson's term as Secretary of State was tainted by these accusations and he never really recovered from his association with Hiss.

The Communist Chinese were very good at self promotion, and several prominent Western visitors to the country became enamored with what they saw in China. One of these was the Dean of Canterbury Cathedral, Dr. Hewlett Johnson, who came back from a visit to China, with praise on what he had seen and heard there. He became to be known as the "Red Dean" to people in the Church of England establishment.

Dean Acheson tried to bolster the "middle forces" who were liberals in China and who did not like the Communists or Nationalists. This was a disaster, since Mao had incorporated many of the "middle forces" ideas into his own philosophy.

Mao Zedong, and the communists, were supported with arms, training and some funds by the Soviets, whereas Chiang Kai-shek, and the nationalists, only saw reduced support from the Truman administration.

When, in 1945, George C Marshall went to China to mediate between the Communists and Nationalists, Marshall knew that the State Department had ordered all aid of arms and ammunition to be held back from the Nationalists. At the same time, the Communists were able to gain vast quantities of arms being surrendered by the Japanese in Manchuria. This placed the Nationalists at a severe disadvantage, but the Truman administration, again, had decided that Asia was not a major area of interest to the US. Europe had to come first.

Even, Douglas MacArthur charged in 1951 that the 1945 Marshall mission to China was one of the greatest **BLUNDERS** in American history, for which the West would pay a heavy price. MacArthur found out firsthand what the loss of China to the Communists would cause in blood. The Korean War (Police Action) would not have happened, if the Nationalists had not been "thrown under the bus" by the lack of foresight by the Truman administration. Truman, Marshall and Acheson lost sight of the global interactions, going on since the end of World War Two. One could not look at one area of the world, with disregard for the effects on other regions of the globe.

Besides the effect of a Communist China on the Korean peninsula, the Vietnam War (undeclared) was also fueled by the flow of arms and equipment from China to the North Vietnamese. Communist China and its effect on the rest of the world, especially the West, is still being felt and "written" today.

5

North Korean Problem
1945-Present

All the current problems on the Korean peninsula began at the end of World War Two, when the Japanese withdrew from the area, after their unconditional surrender. Japan had basically ruled Korea for forty years, ever since the 22nd of August 1904, when the First Japan-Korean Convention treaty was signed. In 1945, at the Yalta and Potsdam conferences, the USSR and the Truman Administration decided that the USSR would occupy the North and the USA would occupy the South, with the division being the 38th parallel. The US agreed to this, because they wanted Russia to enter the war against Japan. In fact, this was not necessary, and it was a give away to Russia, by the US.

On the 6th of August 1945, the first atomic bomb was dropped on Hiroshima, and then, on the 9th of August 1945, the second bomb was dropped on Nagasaki. Russia did not join the war against Japan until the 9th of August 1945, and therefore the Truman administration gave it some spoils of victory that the U.S. did not have to give.

Timeline of Events since Division of Korean Peninsula

DATES	EVENTS
22 August 1910	Korea annexed by Japan under the Japan-Korea Annexation Treaty
4 February 1945	United States and USSR agreed at Yalta to partition Korea along the 38th parallel
14 August 1945	World War II ended with the unconditional surrender of Japan
15 August 1948	The Republic of Korea (ROK) (South Korea) is established and elections held
9 September 1948	The Democratic People's Republic of Korea (North Korea) is established
25 June 1950	North Korea invaded South Korea with the blessing of China and Soviet Union
25 June 1950	UN Security Council meeting, boycotted by the Soviet Union, agreed to send troops
27 June 1950	The United Nations formed command and dispatched armed forces to help South Korea
15 September 1950	The amphibious landing at Inchon drove the North Koreans back up the peninsula
15 October 1950	General MacArthur and President Truman met on Wake Island and discussed strategy
15 October 1950	United Nations Forces entered the North Korean capital Pyongyang
25 November 1950	Chinese offensive took place across the Yalu river driving the UN forces back
11 April 1951	General Douglas MacArthur is relieved of command by U.S. President Harry Truman
13 September 1951	Battle of Heartbreak Ridge began and lasted about thirty days
29 March 1952	President Truman announced he would not run for reelection
23 June 1952	U.S.A.F. bombed the Sui-ho Dam in the North caused power shortages in the North
11 July 1952	U.S. Air Force attacked the North Korean capital Pyongyang
4 November 1952	Former General Eisenhower won the Presidential election in a landslide
27 July 1953	Armistice signed in Panmunjom leaving the border on the 38th parallel as before
9 October 2006	First known nuclear test conducted by North Korea; more have followed
5 April 2009	Satellite launched by long range missile that could be used for nuclear strike

TWILIGHT FOR THE WEST?

The United States, under President Truman, did allow the South to declare its independence on the 15th of August 1948. The South became known as the Republic of Korea. Right after this, on the 9th of September 1948, the USSR, under Stalin, set up the North as a dictatorship, and it became the Democratic People's Republic of Korea (DPRK). Stalin installed Kim Il-sung as the dictator, and the DPRK became a communist country. It had a border with China, which itself became communist in 1949 (see chapter four).

The Soviet forces withdrew from the North in 1948, leaving Kim Il-sung in charge, and the American troops were withdrawn to Japan in 1949, leaving Syngman Rhee as President (24 July 1948 to 26 April 1960) of the Republic of Korea.

The Korean War, described by President Truman as a "police action", started on the 25th of June 1950, when North Korea invaded the South. The South was unprepared for war, and the North pushed the South's forces all the way down to Pusan. Here, they made a stand in the Pusan pocket, until the United Nations troops could get ashore. The United Nations Security Council approved military action (9-0) to save the South. The USSR boycotted the United Nations in January 1950 and left for several months, because the UN would not seat a delegate from Communist China (PRC). This was Joseph Stalin's mistake (**BLUNDER**), for if his representative, Yakov Malik, had attended the June 25th meeting, he could have vetoed the UN military action in Korea. As it was, the UN approved military action, and General Douglas MacArthur was made supreme commander of the troops. At the time, he was in Japan, where he had administered the running of the country, since 1945.

The Truman administration, through Dean Acheson the Secretary of State, indicated that the Korean peninsula was outside the US defense perimeter. This statement probably gave the North Koreans, China and the USSR the idea that they could take over South Korea, and the USA would do nothing. This was **APPEASEMENT** by the US, and it came back to haunt it. Six months later, the North crossed the 38th parallel. In 1950, Dean Acheson (pseudo Neville Chamberlain, see chapter three) also advocated recognizing Communist China. This further encouraged the Chinese to assist North Korea, if needed to prevent their defeat.

General Douglas MacArthur and staff observing the Inchon amphibious landing on the USS Mount McKinley

When the UN troops entered South Korea, they had to land in the Pusan pocket. Under MacArthur's leadership, they started to push the North Korean forces back up the Korean peninsula. MacArthur launched a controversial amphibious landing at Inchon that turned out to be a great success. It cut off many of the North Korean troops and, by the 24th of November 1950, the UN troops had advanced into the North and were close to the Yalu River. This river divided North Korea from China. China decided that it could not allow the Americans to reach the Yalu and sent thousands of Chinese across the river in support of the North.

In the middle of October 1950, MacArthur and Truman met on Wake Island, in the Pacific, to discuss strategy. Although the meeting went fairly well, disagreements soon surfaced, as to how to conduct the war. MacArthur wanted to bomb the Chinese bases on both sides of the Yalu, to stem the tide of Chinese troops. However, Truman, by this time, did not want victory, instead he thought it would be best to negotiate with the Communists. He would not allow MacArthur to bomb the bridges along the Yalu.

President Truman and General MacArthur meet at Wake Island in the Pacific

By the 11th of April 1951, the disagreement between the military and the politicians grew so contentious that Truman finally relieved MacArthur of command and appointed Lt. General Matthew

Ridgeway as commander of the UN forces. MacArthur came home to the US as a hero, and he went before a joint session of Congress to declare amongst other things, that "There is no substitute for Victory".

After having a poor showing in the first Democratic primary of the 1952 election year, President Truman, who was very unpopular, decided not to run again.

Dwight D. Eisenhower ran for President on the Republican ticket and won against Adlai Stevenson in the general election. After he was inaugurated, Eisenhower worked to end the Korean War. The war (police action) continued on, until it finally ended in July 1953, with an armistice. There has never been an actual peace treaty signed, between the North and the South.

Overall, the war flowed back and forth for three years and one month, during which time America lost 33,686 dead, 92,134 wounded and 4759 missing in action. Other members of the United Nations forces also lost many soldiers dead, wounded or MIA.

All these casualties were for what? A Police Action!

When the armistice was signed, on the 27th of July 1953, the demarcation line, between the North and the South, was identical to what it was before the war started - the 38th parallel.

For the next sixty years, North Korea has been run by the Kim family, with support from the Communist Chinese. This **APPEASEMENT** by Truman has led to a rogue country developing nuclear weapons and a long range missile. Once they develop a nuclear device small enough to mount on the missile under development, they will have a weapon with which they can threaten Japan and other Asian countries. In the 1990's, President Clinton tried to appease the North Koreans by offering food and other assistance. However, in the end, the North continued to develop some new weapon systems, including nuclear WMD.

Situation Analysis:

The Truman administration's decisions over China and Korea have had a long lasting effect on the US Affairs of State in the Asian arena. The China issue was discussed in chapter four, therefore only the problems of the Korean peninsula will be covered in this analysis.

The Truman administration's agreement with the USSR to enter the Pacific war, three months after the defeat of Germany, was a major **BLUNDER**. When Truman attended the Potsdam conference (17 July to 2 August, 1945), he already had received word that the US scientists had successfully tested the bomb at Alamogordo, New Mexico, on the 16th of July. The Truman administration should have waited, before encouraging Stalin to enter the war against Japan.

After the USSR did enter the war, they captured some Japanese islands, and Truman had "given" the Soviets the right to occupy the northern half of Korea. This led to the permanent division of Korea, even though there were supposed to be free elections to unify the peninsula.

The Truman administration withdrew the US troops in 1949, leaving South Korea open to Communist aggression. With the Communist Chinese taking over China, Dictator Kim Il sung had major support to attack the South. Dean Acheson's remarks about Korea not being important to the US, further encouraged Kim.

The fact that the USSR boycotted the UN, starting in January 1950, probably saved South Korea. Otherwise, the USSR would have vetoed the Security Council vote to send troops to save the South.

The Truman administration **BLUNDERED** again when it decided that the war was a "police action", and the U.S. wanted a political settlement. After sixty years, America is still waiting for the political settlement and a peace treaty. General MacArthur was considered by some Americans, including Truman, to be somewhat of a prima donna. However, like most generals, his goal in any war or "police action" was victory, but the politicians interfered in the running of this "police action". One of America's most successful generals was relieved of duty, and almost 34,000 American soldiers died for nothing.

The Truman administration's **BLUNDERS** over Korea have resulted in the North Koreans becoming a nuclear power, and a threat to the entire Far East. As long as the Chinese support the North Koreans, the Korean peninsula will remain volatile. The current dictator, Kim Jong-un, appears to be somewhat unpredictable and unstable, and he could be persuaded to take rash action in the future.

6

Hungary
1956

On the 5th of March 1953, Joseph Stalin, the dictator of the Soviet Union, died of a stroke, at the age of seventy-four. His death set off a series of rebellions in Eastern Europe that tested the new masters of the USSR. Just three months after Stalin's death, in June 1953, workers in East Germany rioted and demonstrated against the GDR (German Democratic Republic) communist regime, run by Wilhelm Pieck. The uprising that started in Berlin soon spread to other East German cities and towns. The Russians were stunned by the sudden uprising, but the leaders in Moscow soon got over the shock of it all, and they sent in the Russian tanks, stationed in East Germany.

The Eisenhower administration **BLUNDERED** by hesitating and not having the courage to support the workers, for fear of setting off another war in Europe. Instead, the Americans sent in millions of food parcels, since one of the complaints by the workers was the lack of food. The East German uprising proved that the Republican campaign promises of freeing Eastern

Europe were just words. Thousands of balloons filled with leaflets and Radio Free Europe encouraged the uprising, but when the workers expected support from the West, none came. The uprising was crushed by the Soviets, and the lesson of what happens to freedom loving, Eastern Europeans was seen by all of the captive nations.

On the 25th of February 1956, Nikita Khrushchev, then head of the Soviet Union, gave a speech to the 20th Communist Party Congress, in which he criticized Joseph Stalin and his cult of the personality that was alien to the philosophy of Marxism-Leninism. Stalin used the Russian mass media, propaganda and other methods to create an image that idolized him and made him look heroic. Photographs had been doctored to make Stalin look like the savior of the revolution. He also used the propaganda to make him have a worshipful image, through unquestioning flattery and praise. He also became the person who saved Russia during WWII. Besides Stalin, Hitler and some Roman emperors also created a cult of the personality to make themselves look god like.

Although his words were not broadcast to the Soviet Union or the Eastern Bloc, word about the speech leaked out, and it provided encouragement to nationalists in the East European countries. On the 29th of June 1956, Polish workers in Poznań went on strike, but the Polish Communist authorities quickly put down the labor unrest, with their troops and imposed martial law. A new leader by the name of Gomulka took over, and he made some reforms to increase the standard of living, for the average Pole.

Timeline of Events for the Hungarian Revolt

DATES	EVENTS
27 February 1949	Hungary became a Peoples Republic and Matyas Rakosi headed the Communist party
5 March 1953	Joseph Stalin, dictator of the Soviet Union for about thirty years died of a stroke
4 July 1953	Imre Nagy became Prime Minister of the Hungarian Government for the first time
25 February 1956	Khrushchev criticized Joseph Stalin, raised hopes of reform minded communist politicians
23 October 1956	Students demonstrated in the street of Budapest, marched to capital's radio station
24 October 1956	Imre Nagy became Prime Minister of the Hungarian Government again
25 October 1956	Soviet tanks opened fire and started to shoot unarmed protestors
28 October 1956	New government sworn in and reforms promised by Imre Nagy
29 October 1956	Israel invaded the Sinai as part of the secret agreement with France and Britain
30 October 1956	Hungarian Cardinal Mindszenty is released from prison and Soviet troops withdrew
31 October 1956	Nagy broadcasts that Hungary would withdraw from the Warsaw Pact
1 November 1956	Kádár left government and formed rival government in East Hungary with Soviet help
2 November 1956	Soviet Ambassador Andropov asked to inform his government that Hungarians wanted talks
3 November 1956	KGB Head Heneral Ivan Serov orders arrest of Hungarian delegation for the negotiations
4 November 1956	Soviet Union forces including tanks invaded Hungary and started crushing the revolution
4 November 1956	Imre Nagy was removed from power by the Soviets and replaced with János Kádár
11 November 1956	Fighting in Budapest died down and USSR claimed victory over freedom fighters
22 November 1956	Imre Nagy left the Yugoslav Embassy and was immediately arrested and taken to Romania
16 June 1958	Imre Nagy executed by hanging after being convicted in a secret trial, as an example

The next country to go through an uprising experience was Hungary. On the 23rd of October 1956, students in Budapest, the capital of Hungary, took to the streets, after issuing their sixteen points' document. The students called for personal freedom, greater availability of food and abolishment of the secret police (AVH). The students tried to break in to Radio Budapest to broadcast their demands, but were denied entry by the AVH. Attempting to disperse the students, the AVH opened fire on the crowd.

The next day, battles raged in the streets of Budapest, and Imre Nagy was reinstated as Prime Minister, with a János Kádár being appointed as Foreign Minister. Cardinal József Mindszenty, an anti-Communist and anti-Nazi, was also released from prison where he was serving a life sentence for treason. He had been sentenced to prison in 1949.

Imre Nagy,
Hungarian Prime
Minister in 1953
and 1956

By the 26th of October 1956, the revolution had spread to the Hungarian countryside, and Imre Nagy told the Soviets that he wanted to negotiate a withdrawal of Soviet forces. After Nagy was sworn in as Prime Minister, he went on the national radio, promising withdrawal of Soviet troops, and the disbandment of the secret police. The border with Western Europe was opened up, and Hungarians fled to the West through Austria. Initially, the flood of refugees was small, but it increased rapidly, when the Soviets started to crack down on the freedom fighters. The Hungarians expected help from America and other Western countries, but it never came. Radio Free Europe urged the Hungarians to stand firm and fight until help could arrive, but it never came.

By the 1st of November 1956, Hungary announced it was withdrawing from the Warsaw Pact and that Hungary was now neutral. This was too much for the Soviets and, on the 4th of November, they invaded with an estimated 1,000 tanks and entered the capital, where heavy fighting took place. Nagy broadcast an appeal on the radio at 5:15 am, but soon the radio station was silenced by the Soviet forces. It is estimated that 5,000 Hungarian freedom fighters were killed and over 200,000 Hungarians fled to the West, mainly through Austria. The United Nations called for the Soviets to withdraw, but this demand was ignored by the Russians. Many buildings in Budapest were destroyed and, Cardinal Mindszenty sought refuge in the U.S. embassy. He remained there for fifteen years, before he was allowed to leave Hungary.

By the 11th of November 1956, the Soviets declared victory and appointed János Kádár as Prime Minister. It is estimated that approximately 700 hundred Soviet forces were killed either by the freedom fighters or execution, for refusing to fight. Imre Nagy sought refuge in the Yugoslav Embassy, and after being guaranteed of safe passage to return to his home, he was arrested and taken to Romania. Two years later, he was tried in a secret trial, found guilty of treason and then hung. He was executed on Kremlin orders, so as to set an example to other East European bloc leaders, who might think about breaking away from the Soviet Bloc.

Destroyed Soviet tank in Budapest

Photo by Ismeretien

János Kádár was the leader of Hungary from 1956 to 1988, when he resigned. Initially, he rounded up many liberals, agitators and freedom fighters that supported the revolution and either imprisoned or executed them. Later, he relaxed his rigid control, once he was firmly in power. After he resigned in 1988, more reforms were initiated, and by June 1989, a government of national unity was formed. The Soviet Union withdrew all their armed forces by 1991, when the new Russia Federation was created. Imre Nagy was rehabilitated, given a state funeral and then reburied with full national honors.

Situation Analysis:

First, the East German uprising in 1953, then the Polish workers strike in June 1956, and finally the Hungarian revolution gave the United States, under President Eisenhower, the opportunity to support and provide aid to freedom loving citizens of Eastern Europe. Radio Free Europe encouraged these uprisings with their broadcasts, but then no support was forthcoming. This was a **BLUNDER** on the West's part, especially the United States. The Iron Curtain may have come down a lot sooner than in 1989, if the West had acted.

Nikita Khrushchev took the American response to these revolts to mean that the United States and the West were not willing to use military force or supply material aid, to the Eastern Europe countries controlled by the Soviets. Khrushchev then went ahead a few years later in 1961 and had the Berlin Wall installed. He figured again that the U.S. would do nothing, especially with the new, inexperienced President Kennedy.

U. S. President
Dwight D.
Eisenhower
1953-1961

In the fall of 1956, the British, French and Israelis invaded Egypt, and this was unfortunate, since it happened at the same time that the Soviets crushed the Hungarian uprising. Colonel Nasser, the Egyptian leader, had nationalized the Suez Canal on the 26th of July 1956. On the 31st of October 1956, the British and French started the operation with a bombing campaign in and around the Suez Canal. Although the British and French were succeeding in their military goals, they were forced to agree to a ceasefire on the 6th of November, by the Americans. The Eisenhower administration had threatened economic and oil sanctions, unless they withdrew. The operation was a military victory but a political **BLUNDER**.

The handling of the two crises turned into a major **BLUNDER** for the Eisenhower administration. Some statesmen claimed that the United Nations, at this point in time, was turned from a strong voice for international law, into a bloviating (debating) society. The UN was unable to prevent the invasion of Hungary by the Soviet Union. There were plenty of speeches by the members, but no action. The Suez Canal fiasco, and the reaction of America, taught any would be dictator that inappropriate action would be overlooked by the UN and the West.

The fact that America would come down hard on her friends, and not do anything against their enemies, was a powerful lesson to all countries; friend or foe. As a result of this hypocritical response, France decided to pull out of NATO and go it alone, since they felt they could not trust the Americans. The Soviets, as mentioned previously, saw the American response as an "invitation" for Russia to do whatever they wanted in Eastern Europe. Thirteen years later, the Czechs tried to obtain freedom, and they, in turn, were crushed by the Soviets. Again, the West did nothing, as outlined in chapter ten of this book.

7

Cuba
1959-1961

Cuba was freed, with American assistance, from Spanish domination in 1898. The conflict was known as the Spanish-American War, and it ended in the same year, with the signing of the Treaty of Paris. After a three year occupation by the American army, Cuba became somewhat free. An education program, initiated by the Americans, was at first a success, but the subject of racism kept cropping up. By 1952, the dream of a free Cuba (Cuba Libre) was unrealized, and Batista became the dictator of the island. Corruption became widespread, and the U.S. crime syndicates flourished on the island. The island deteriorated into chaos, and the U.S. government withdrew support of Batista in 1958.

Fidel Castro understood the plight of the poor and the lack of a good education system. His revolution, in the name of José Martí who was a national hero to most Cubans, was enticing to the countries poor and the 26th of July movement gathered strength. José Martí, who was a Cuban and lived from 1853-1895, promoted liberty and political independence from Spain and America. By the 1st of January 1959, Batista fled the island with his millions of dollars, and Fidel Castro took over the government. In the beginning, he did not declare that he was creating a Communist state and, on the 7th of January 1959, the United States recognized the new government. Over the next few months, there began to arise some conflicts, between the Eisenhower administration and Fidel Castro's government. By April, Castro talked more like a Communist dictator, than a freedom loving Cuban. On the 8th of July, the CIA issued a briefing for the NSC, reporting about some preparations by the Cubans, to subvert the Dominican Republic.

From then on, the U.S. started to prepare plans to remove the Castro government from power. The feeling by the Eisenhower administration was that the U.S. could not afford to have a full blown Communist State in the Western Hemisphere, let alone ninety miles from Florida. In late October 1959, Eisenhower approved a plan to support exiled Cuban elements, with the intent of causing the downfall of Fidel Castro. Around the same time, Castro organized a meeting of Cuban officials where he laid out a plan for the state to take over just about every organization in Cuba; in other words, create a communist state.

In early December, a group of exiled Cubans met to discuss actions that could be taken to cause the overthrow of Castro. In January 1960, bombing missions were started and sabotage took place by anti–Castro elements in Cuba. In February 1960, the MRR (Movimiento de Recuperación Revolucionaria) released a manifesto, calling for the overthrow of the Castro communist regime and the creation of a Christian democratic government. On the 18th of February 1960, in response to this anti-Castro activity, the Cuban government nationalized all U. S. businesses in Cuba and gave the companies no compensation.

On the 28th of September 1960, the CIA attempted to drop a supply of arms to guerrillas in Cuba, but it turned out to be a disaster, because most of the arms were not dropped in the correct location. On the 31st of October 1960, the CIA created a plan to train a minimum of 1500 Cubans in Guatemala. Just a week later, on the 8th of November, the CIA formed a group, called the Brigade 2506, and changed the overall plan from sabotage, to an amphibious landing on the Cuban coast. The overall goal of the CIA plan was to hold some Cuban territory, declare a new government and encourage the Cuban population to join the revolt.

On the 12th of December 1960, a campaign of dropping, by aircraft and balloons, propaganda leaflets on Cuba began. In January 1961, recruitment of exiles, in Florida and other areas, for the invasion was increased significantly. The invasion plan that had been approved by the Eisenhower administration was turned over to the incoming Kennedy administration. John F. Kennedy was personally briefed about the plan, just two days after his inauguration, and he was urged to support the overthrow of the Castro communist regime, established in the Americas. A critical part of the plan was the air support required to cover the actual landing on the coast and the protection of the supply ships waiting offshore. The invasion was scheduled to start on the 15th of April 1961, just three months into the Kennedy administration's tenure.

TWILIGHT FOR THE WEST?

Timeline of Events Leading Up to Cuba

DATES	EVENTS
10 March 1952	General Batista became dictator of Cuba after serving as president in the 1940s
1 January 1959	The Cuban dictator Batista fled Cuba with a personal fortune and ended up in Portugal
1 January 1959	Fidel Castro took over Cuba after a rebellion that forced General Batista from office
7 January 1959	United States Government recognized the new Cuban government under Castro
19 April 1959	Fidel Castro visited the U.S. for first time and held talks with U.S. government
Late October 1959	President Eisenhower approved plan to support Cubans opposed to Castro
8 November 1960	Senator Kennedy defeated V.P. Richard Nixon in presidential election
20 January 1961	President Kennedy took office and received plans for the Bay of Pigs invasion
15 April 1961	Eight B-26 bombers took off from Nicaragua to attack the Cuba and it's air force
16 April 1961	Kennedy administration canceled follow up air raids. CIA realized Cuban rebels doomed
17 April 1961	1400 Cuban exiles (Brigade 2506) landed in Cuba but supply ships sunk by Cuba.
18 April 1961	The Brigade started to run out of ammo and Kennedy administration refused to help
19 April 1961	Brigade 2506 collapsed and took refuge. JFK tried to figure out how to recover
24 May 1961	Tractors for Freedom program took hold by private citizens to free Cubans
4 June 1961	President Kennedy met with Nikita Khrushchev in Vienna, Austria
13 August 1961	East Germany with Khrushchev okay sealed off East Berlin and East Germany from West
15 October 1962	US U2 flight confirmed MRBM missiles installed in Cuba by the USSR
22 October 1962	Kennedy Administration announced naval blockade around Cuba
28 October1962	Khrushchev agreed to withdraw missiles if Kennedy agreed to withdraw Turkish missiles
28 October 1962	The U.S. Government officially ended the naval blockade of Cuba

Somehow, the U.S. press heard of this planned invasion and publicized it, causing great anguish for Kennedy and his government. This leak warned Castro of the impending invasion, and he laid plans to counteract it. However, the planning for the invasion continued, and the Voice of America increased its broadcasts into Cuba, encouraging the people to rise up, against their communist dictator.

The action started Saturday morning, on the 15th of April 1961, with an aerial bombing attack by a flight of B-26B Marauder planes with FAR (Fuerza Aérea Revolucionaria) markings, on Castro's air force. The B-26s took off from an airfield in Guatemala, and they flew over the Gulf of Mexico. The attack was not a complete success, and some of Castro's fighter aircraft escaped being destroyed.

The next day, the 16th of April, Fidel Castro announced that Cuba was officially a Communist state, while attending a funeral for the Cubans killed in the air raids on the previous day. In the evening, President Kennedy cancelled additional air raids, on Cuban airfields for political reasons. In fact, according to a firsthand report from a USAF pilot who had taken off from a Florida airbase in a Wing of Lockheed F104s, he reported that as he winged his way towards Cuba to help the rebels, his flight was called back. Because President Kennedy cancelled the air support, which the Brigade 2506 invasion strategy relied on, it meant that the invasion in the Bay of Pigs would almost surely fail.

As planned, early on Monday morning of the 17th of April 1961, the Brigade 2506 landed on the south coast of Cuba, at the Bay of Pigs, and it almost immediately came under attack, from the Cuban planes that survived the attack two days before. If the follow up raid had not been cancelled by Kennedy, these planes in all likelihood would have been destroyed on the ground. Two supply ships, on which the invaders depended for weapons and ammunition, were sunk

On the 18th of April, the Cuban exiles started to run out of ammunition and hope. They were still stuck on the beach, and they had not taken enough territory, where they could claim to have established a new government. The leaders of the Brigade appealed for help from the American warships that were close by. Again, President Kennedy took the side of politics, and he refused permission for the U.S. Navy to go into action.

By the 19th of April, five days after the first B26 bombing, the Cuban exiles were out of options and ammunition. They fled into the swamps near the Bay of Pigs, where they were forced out by the Cuban military. They were taken prisoner, and Castro gloated about how he had defeated the Americans. It was estimated that about 1200 of The Brigade 2506 were captured and imprisoned. A program called "Tractors for Freedom" was promoted by Eleanor Roosevelt (FDRs widow), and others, to free the prisoners, to no avail. All the prisoners were tried and convicted; some were executed and the others sentenced to long prison sentences.

Finally, in December 1962, a year and a half after the Bay of Pigs invasion, and after the Cuban missile crisis was resolved, a deal was made between the U.S. and Cuba for the release of the remaining 1,113 prisoners. It amounted to the donation of food and medicine, at the value of $53 million, which was given to the Castro regime. The food and medicine was supplied by private companies and did not involve the U.S. government. Thus ended the sordid invasion of Cuba; named the Bay of Pigs.

Situation Analysis:

The Cuban crisis that started in 1959 with the Castro rebellion, against the Batista regime, has continued for fifty-five years. The Eisenhower administration threw Batista under the proverbial bus because his regime was viewed as corrupt. Fidel Castro and his 26th of July movement were misunderstood by the U.S. intelligence community. For some unknown reason, the U.S. thought by withdrawing support of Batista, it would prevent Fidel Castro from obtaining victory. This **BLUNDER** by the Eisenhower government created an opportunity, for enemies of the dictator Batista, to take advantage of the situation in Cuba. Fidel Castro understood the plight of Cuba's poor and used this understanding to encourage fighters to join his organization.

After Castro caused Batista to flee Cuba in early 1959, the Eisenhower administration recognized that Castro was going to be a continuing problem in the Americas. Under the direction of the White House, the CIA and U.S. military started to develop plans to overthrow the Castro government. The Eisenhower administration believed that they could reverse the

BLUNDER of the previous year. The plan revolved around a four part strategy.

First, a considerable number of Cuban exiles would be enlisted and trained in military tactics. This would be done in Guatemala so as not to involve directly the U.S. Government. Guatemala, at the time, was friendly with the U.S. Second, the Cuban air force would be destroyed on the ground by B-26B marauders armed with high explosive bombs. There were still many B26s around from World War Two and the markings would be changed to the Fuerza Aérea Revolucionaria insignia. Third, after this destruction of the Cuban Air Force was attained, an invasion of the Cuban southern coast could be accomplished with landing craft and freighters loaded with arms and ammunition. Lastly, once ashore, the rebels would seize as much territory as possible and declare the establishment of a new government. The U.S. could then openly recognize the government and support it.

One key feature of the actual invasion was that the U.S. would provide air cover with unmarked planes for the landing, if it was required. Secrecy of the entire plan was of the utmost importance so that Castro did not get wind of it. However, in October 1960, Castro did receive intelligence of the training camps in Guatemala and so he knew something was planned, but did not know the actual timing.

When the Kennedy administration took over in January 1961, it had already been briefed about the plan before inauguration. In February 1961, Kennedy approved the plan, but when it actually commenced, he committed the next **BLUNDER** of the Cuba crisis and would not allow the air cover, by unmarked U.S. planes. This caused the invasion fleet to be attacked by the remaining Cuban Air Force and the whole plan collapsed.

Many politicians considered Kennedy a novice at power politics, and that he did not understand the relationships between various global problems. His ambivalence in the Cuban crisis set up the next problem with Khrushchev. The two held a summit meeting in Vienna where Kennedy was outsmarted by Khrushchev, at every move. Khrushchev came away from the Summit with the view that he could "run over" Kennedy, any time he wanted.

Two months after the Vienna Summit, Khrushchev created a crisis in Berlin, by having Walter Ulbricht install the Berlin Wall. Khrushchev instructions were that if the Americans knocked down the wall in the first forty eight hours, the East Germans were to do nothing. Kennedy and his administration did nothing, and the Wall stayed erect for almost thirty years. Only then did Kennedy get some backbone, when he blockaded the Soviet ships during the Cuban missile crisis of late 1962. The two **BLUNDERS** have allowed Castro to stay in power for years.

8

Berlin
1961

In less than two months after the Bay of Pigs fiasco, and one year after the 1960 Paris summit collapsed, because of the U2 spy plane incident, a two-day meeting was held in Vienna, at the beginning of June 1961, between Nikita Khrushchev and John F. Kennedy.   One of the problems with this meeting, right from the start, was that there was no specific agenda.   It was supposed to be an informal meeting between the two superpower leaders, to discuss issues of common interest.

President John Kennedy and Nikita Khrushchev at Vienna summit meeting

Khrushchev came to the summit with years of political infighting and having survived several Stalin purges. Kennedy, on the other hand, was a Congressman from 1947 to 1953, U.S. senator for almost eight years and President for six months. He had never governed a state, where one has to give and take, all the time. Kennedy was also coming to the negotiations with the first major failure of his presidency, just a few months before. The matter of Cuba, with the failed invasion at the Bay of Pigs, demonstrated to Khrushchev that he was dealing with a neophyte and an amateur, in the art of international politics.

Khrushchev came to the Vienna meeting, wanting to discuss the problem of West Berlin that lay within the communist Democratic Republic of Germany (GDR). He also wanted to discuss the cold war issues of nuclear weapons and regional conflicts, including Laos and Cuba. Kennedy did not appear to have a clear agenda for the meeting, and he ignored recommendations from his cabinet, not to get into an ideological debate with the Soviet leader. In addition, Kennedy's advisors believed he should not meet with the Soviet leader, so soon after his election to the U.S. Presidency.

On the 3rd of June 1961, Kennedy and Khrushchev met for the first time, at the residence of the U.S. ambassador to Austria. On the second day, June 4th, another meeting was held at the Soviet Embassy, in Vienna. Kennedy was shocked at Khrushchev's tone, on most of the subjects discussed.

There was total disagreement when the subject of Germany, and specifically Berlin, was addressed. Khrushchev wanted a peace treaty with Germany that would turn over control of access to Berlin to the GDR. This Kennedy would not agree to it, and Khrushchev threatened to sign a peace treaty unilaterally with the GDR, by the end of 1961. The reason that the Soviets and the East Germans were so keen on this treaty was because over three million, East Germans had fled to the West, from 1945 to 1961. Most of these refugees were professional people, such as scientists, teachers, etc. This amounted to a massive brain drain on the GDR, and Walter Ulbricht, the GDR leader, was concerned that if it continued, it would create instability in the GDR. Eventually, it could lead to the GDR being ungovernable, without enough educated people to staff the various organizations.

Even before the Vienna summit, Erich Honecker, a protégé of Walter Ulbricht, had been ordering and storing construction material to build the Berlin Wall, if it was required. This material was ordered from several companies, so as not to attract attention with one large order. In addition, the material was stored around the GDR, in various warehouses, so as not to be noticed.

During one session of the Vienna summit, Khrushchev became heartened by Kennedy, when he seemed to give silent approval for some kind of control, to stop East German refugees attempting to go to the West. The Soviet leader took it that the United States would not oppose a Wall being built.

On the 15th of June 1961, Walter Ulbricht gave a speech to the International Press Conference, in which he stressed that East Germany had no intention of building a Wall. This statement was strange, because a Wall had never been mentioned before. He also called for the neutralization of West Berlin.

Initially, Khruschev was against the Wall, due to the possibility of hostilities with the West. However, two weeks later Nikita Khrushchev changed his mind. Obviously, President Kennedy's tacit approval, and his lack of negotiating skills, had its influence on the Soviet leader. The whole issue of Berlin, and its position inside the East German boundaries, was of major concern to the Soviets.

On the 1st of August 1961, a meeting was held in Moscow, between Khrushchev and Ulbricht, to discuss the Wall. Since 1952, the border between East and West Germany had been sealed off, and only in Berlin was the border porous. Ulbricht stressed to Khrushchev that if he wanted to save East Germany, he would have to agree to the Wall being built. Ulbricht convinced Khrushchev that the Wall had to be built soon.

In fact, in some planning by the East Germans, led by Erich Honecker, it was decided that a weekend would be the best time to construct the wall, and that the weekend of August 12, 13 would be ideal. After considerable discussion and persuasion by Ulbricht, Khrushchev finally gave his approval, and Ulbricht returned to Germany, to finalize the plans for the Wall. Khrushchev, however, was still concerned about the reaction of the West, particularly the Americans.

TWILIGHT FOR THE WEST?

Timeline of Events Leading Up to the Berlin Wall

DATES	EVENTS
8 May 1945	World War Two ended in Europe with Germany divided into four zones
24 June 1948	Berlin airlift is initiated by the US after the Russians closed the corridor into Berlin
12 May 1949	The Soviets ended the blockade the day before and the Berlin Airlift ended
23 May 1949	Federal Republic of Germany is formed combining the US, French and British zones
7 October 1949	German Democratic Republic officially started to function with Soviet approval
16 June 1953	East Berlin construction workers go on strike and demonstrated against GDR government
17 June 1953	Soviets tanks and troops put down uprising with scores of workers killed or executed
1954 - 1960	There was a massive "brain drain" of engineers, teachers and doctors
1 May 1960	An American U2 reconnaissance plane, with pilot Gary Powers, shot down over Russia
16 May 1960	Paris Summit meeting between US, USSR, France and Britain collapsed in disarray
3 June 1961	Start of summit meeting between Khrushchev and Kennedy in Vienna, Austria
4 June 1961	End of summit meeting between Khrushchev and Kennedy in Vienna, Austria
April to August1961	East Germany started to stockpile materials for building the wall
1 August 1961	Contact between Khrushchev and Ulbricht took place and Khrushchev approved the wall
12 August 1961	A Döllnsee meeting of top East German officials took place and wall given OK
13 August 1961	East Germany with Khrushchev blessing sealed off East Berlin and East Germany from West
16 August 1961	East German workers started erecting a solid wall 6 feet high to replace barbed wire
26 June 1963	Kennedy visited the Berlin Wall and in its shadow stated Ich bin ein Berliner
12 June 1987	Ronald Reagan visited the wall and says " Mr. Gorbachev, tear down this wall"
9 November 1989	Berlin Wall came down after Gorbachev decided not to support the GDR any longer

On the 12th of August 1961, at a garden party meeting of top East German officials at Döllnsee, Ulbricht announced the construction of the Wall and signed the necessary orders. This Wall was a surprise to many of the attendees, so well had the Wall been kept secret. However, there had been a leak, from an unnamed source, that had been provided to the US Military Intelligence. However, this intelligence report did not get to the correct US people in time, for contingency plans to be made.

At midnight of the 12th of August, the East Germans started to string barbed wire across the entire border, between East and West Berlin. When Berliners woke up Sunday morning, the Wall was fait accompli (an accomplished fact). Lines of East German worker militia men, with weapons, faced into East Berlin, to scare off any would be refugees to the West. One fact, which was not apparent to passersby, was that these militia men had no ammunition in their weapons. In fact, Khrushchev was so concerned about the Wall causing an armed conflict, or even a war, that the order was given that if the Americans broke through the barbed wire fence in the first forty-eight hours, the Russian and East German troops were not to fight back. The Americans acquiesced and did not challenge or attempt to knock down the wall.

Three days later, on the 16th of August 1961, the East Germans started to construct a permanent wall made of concrete and blocks, six feet high, with barbed wire on top. East German guards were issued ammunition and told to shoot any East German that tried to escape over or though the Wall.

In October 1961, friction between the U.S. and the Soviets increased, when an American diplomat Albert Hensing probed the border, between East and West Berlin. Under the rules set down in Potsdam at the end of World War Two, the United States had the right for its personnel (Also British and French) to move freely, through any sector of Berlin. Hensing was delayed by East German guards, which was against the rules. Only Soviet forces were supposed to patrol the border. East German police had no authority to stop or delay American personnel.

On the 27th of October 1961, there was a confrontation between American and Russian tanks, with live ammunition, at the border between East and West Berlin. In telephone conversations, between Kennedy and Khrushchev, it was agreed both sides would withdraw their tanks, one at a time. The crisis was resolved without bloodshed or war. However, by the end of 1961, it was obvious that the Soviets had achieved their objective; the sealing of the border between East and West Berlin.

Situation Analysis:

For President Kennedy who was elected in November 1960, the year 1961 started out with great promise and of course "Camelot". However, it did not take long for "the bloom to fall off the rose". Three months into his presidency, the Bay of Pigs fiasco took place in Cuba. The Kennedy administration **BLUNDERED,** when it cancelled the air cover for the invasion landing by the Cuban exiles. A few days later, after supply ships had been sunk, the invasion collapsed and the Brigade 2506 members were captured.

Then President Kennedy **BLUNDERED** when he went to Vienna, two months after the Cuban fiasco, and met with Nikita Khrushchev to discuss international matters, concerning the communist and free worlds. Kennedy's advisors recommended that it would not be prudent to meet with the Soviet leader, so soon after his inauguration and the Bay of Pigs disaster. He went anyway and Nikita Khrushchev treated Kennedy, as a harsh school teacher admonishes a delinquent student.

President Kennedy basically gave Khrushchev a green light to build the Wall in East Berlin, as long as he did not try to negate the West's right to be in West Berlin. This **APPEASEMENT** by Kennedy gave the Soviet leader an assurance that the West would do nothing to stop the Wall being built.

Two months after the summit in Vienna, the Berlin Wall was built and, even as a precaution by Khrushchev, the East German and Russian troops were given orders not to challenge the West, if they attempted to knock down the Wall, within the first forty-eight hours. The Kennedy administration did nothing, and the Wall remained in place for the next twenty-eight years.

In August 1961, the Kennedy administration did recognize the seriousness of the issues in Berlin and announced the buildup of conventional forces in Europe. This expansion of U.S. forces caused the Soviet leader to realize that he could not sign a peace treaty, with East Germany, without risking a limited or all out war in Europe.

Finally in October of 1961, the United States did challenge the right of East Germans to limit access by America, British and French troops to enter all sectors of Berlin, including the East. Under the Potsdam agreement, only Russian troops could ask to see American credentials to verify who they were. East Berlin police or border guards could not do so.

The final fallout from the events of 1961 was the Cuban missile crisis in the fall of 1962. Castro had requested that the Soviets place missiles in Cuba to deter any future invasion by Cuban exiles or even Americans. In July 1962, after much discussion, Khrushchev agreed to station some nuclear missiles on the island, and the USSR started to ship them there, under wraps, on Russian ships. The world came close to a nuclear war, because of the blunders and appeasement in 1961. The Soviets finally agreed to withdraw the missiles in November 1962, after the US agreed to withdraw their missiles from Turkey and promised not to invade Cuba.

President Kennedy was assassinated one year later in November 1963 by Lee Harvey Oswald.

Khrushchev won a lot more than he lost, for the Soviets, but to other members of the Soviet leadership, the events caused them to realize Khrushchev was too brash, dangerous and unreliable. In just under two years after the Cuban missile crisis, he was removed from office in October 1964 and allowed to retire to the country.

9

Vietnam
1954-1975

Japan formally surrendered on the 2nd of September 1945, after the bombing of Hiroshima and Nagasaki, and World War Two came to an end. Japanese soldiers on the Asian mainland returned home. As the Japanese withdrew, the French returned to Indochina and reclaimed their colonies of Vietnam, Laos and Cambodia. However, in Vietnam, there was a nationalist/communist leader, named Ho Chi Minh, who had led an earlier revolt and wanted independence for Vietnam.

On the 19th of December 1946, Ho Chi Minh declared war on the French Union, after he realized that the French would not allow Vietnam to gain its independence. This date is considered, by politicians and statesmen, to be the start of the Indochina War. The USSR and China recognized Ho Chi Minh's government in January 1950, as the legitimate ruling body of Vietnam. In February 1950, Ho Chi Minh travelled to Moscow, where he met with Stalin and Mao Zedong, to discuss aid for his struggle, against the French colonial rulers.

TWILIGHT FOR THE WEST?

Ho waged a guerilla war against the French for eight long years, before it ended in 1954, at the Battle of Dien Bien Phu. The French had been slowly withdrawing from their overseas colonies since the end of World War Two, due to the expense of maintaining them. The French Expeditionary Corps, located at an old Japanese WWII base, came under bombardment from Viet Minh guns in the hills. These guns surrounded the French in this North Vietnamese town, called Dien Bien Phu, near the Laos border. The siege lasted from the 13th of March to the 7th of May 1954, and it resulted in a major defeat for the French. The battle was similar to the World War One trench warfare, with massive casualties.

Two months later, after the defeat of the French at this town, the warring parties came to an agreement, and the accords were signed on the 21st of July 1954. The French agreed to pull out of Indochina, and they evacuated Hanoi on the 9th of October 1954. On the 20th of May 1955, the French departed Saigon and retreated to a few coastal bases. Finally, on the 28th of April 1956, the last French troops left Vietnam for good.

During the French defense at Dien Bien Phu, a few American pilots, flying B26s, had flown covert bombing missions in support of the French, but they did not have much effect on the outcome of the battle. The Eisenhower administration did not want to openly support the French war effort, as the President felt that America should not be drawn into a war, on the Asian mainland. Just a year before, Eisenhower had managed to halt the Korean War (police action).

Under the Geneva Accord of 1954, Vietnam was divided into two areas, with two leaders; Ho Chi Minh and Ngo Dinh Diem. Elections were supposed to be held in order to unify the country, under one government. This election never took place, and guerilla fighting between the North and the South soon commenced. The United States sent advisors to the South, to help in the training of their troops. The North was supported by the Communist Chinese that had just won in the civil war against Chiang Kai-shek, a few years earlier.

In 1961, President Kennedy came into office, and he continued to support the military advisor program, already in place. On the 2nd of November 1963, the Kennedy administration covertly approved the assassination of the South Vietnam President, Ngo Dinh Diem. Ho Chi Minh is said to have stated that this was a major mistake on America's part, and he thought it would make his plan to take over the South a lot easier. Three weeks later, President Kennedy himself was assassinated in Dallas, by Lee Harvey Oswald.

The assassinated South Vietnamese leader, Ngo Dinh Diem, was a Roman Catholic, and he had many conflicts with the Buddhist population and religious leaders. The problem was that after the military coup and assassination of Ngo Dinh Diem, there was severe infighting amongst the South Vietnamese generals. For some time, no effective leader for the South Vietnamese, to rally around, came forward. Finally, after a couple of years, a general by the name of

Nguyễn Văn Thiêu became President, and the political situation calmed down.

The guerillas in the South were named the Viet Cong, and they were supported by the North Vietnamese, with arms and training. The Viet Cong aim was to overthrow the South Vietnamese government.

On the 2nd of August 1964, the USS Maddox was on an intelligence signals spying mission, close to North Vietnam. The North Vietnamese claimed it was in their territorial waters, while the U.S. claimed it was in international waters. The demarcation line was in dispute, ever since the Geneva accords of 1954. However, three North Vietnamese torpedo boats attacked the Maddox and were driven off. The Maddox claimed the North Vietnamese fired first, but in fact it appears the Maddox fired first. The gunners on the U.S. ship had been told to fire on any target, within a range of ten thousand yards.

Two days later, on the 4th of August 1964, the USS Maddox was again on patrol, when it supposedly came under attack. This was later shown to be false, but it was used as a pretext to get a resolution through Congress. The NSA (National Security Agency) claimed the second Tonkin Gulf attack may have involved ghosts on the radar, not actual torpedo boats. On the 10th of August 1964, a joint resolution of Congress, named "The Southeast Asia Resolution" (H.J. Resolution 1145), was passed by Congress and signed by President Johnson. It allowed the President to conduct military operations in Southeast Asia, without the benefit of a declaration of war.

Timeline of Events Involving Vietnam

DATES	EVENTS
14 August 1945	World War Two ended and Japanese forces withdrew soon thereafter
22 September 1945	The French and their army returned to Vietnam and reestablished colonial rule.
8 March 1949	French recognized emperor Bao Dai as head of an independent State of Vietnam
13 March 1954	Battle of Dien Bien Phu started between the French forces and the Viet Minh
7 May 1954	Battle for Dien Bien Phu ended with defeat of the French Expeditionary Corps
20 July 1954	Geneva Accords divided Vietnam at 17th parallel. The U.S. and South refused to sign
1 January 1955	The U.S., under Eisenhower, started supplying the South with military aid
21 December 1961	The first United States combat soldier was killed in combat
1 November 1963	Ngo Dinh Diem was executed after a military coup ousted him from power the day before
22 November 1963	U.S. President John F Kennedy was assassinated in Dallas by Lee Harvey Oswald
7 August 1964	Gulf of Tonkin Resolution passed by Congress
10 August 1964	US President Lyndon Baines Johnson signed the Gulf of Tonkin resolution
9 February 1965	Us troops started to be deployed in Vietnam in support of South Vietnam troops
30 January 1968	Viet Cong launched TET offensive and caused havoc in South Vietnam
25 January 1969	Paris peace talks opened between the United States, North and South Vietnam
22 July 1971	United States Senate passed resolution calling for withdrawal of troops
11 August 1972	Last American ground troops departed leaving only airmen and medical personnel
27 January 1973	Paris Peace Accords are signed signaling the start of the end of the war for America
29 March 1973	Last American combat troops are withdrawn from Vietnam
30 April; 1975	Last Americans left South Vietnam with the evacuation of the US Embassy

From August 1964 to August 1973, this police action (second Indochina war) caused the deaths of 58,300 U.S. military personnel, 153,303 wounded and 1641 MIAs. The war was marked by bombing raids into North Vietnam, Cambodia and Laos, in order to eliminate infiltration trails and strategic military locations in the North. No real, overt effort was made during the nine years to win the war or infiltrate north of the demarcation line; the 17th parallel.

There were many problems in the running of the war by the military. One of them was that the U.S. generals were not given the authority to win the war, but just "hold the line" (the 17th parallel). In addition, the "war" was waged from Washington. The White House picked the targets to be bombed, not the military on the front line. This was akin to the American Revolution, two hundred years earlier, where the American guerillas were fighting a far superior force, being directed by London five thousand miles away (three months by boat for orders to arrive).

Two years after the American troop withdrawal from South Vietnam, the South collapsed and was taken over by the North. Finally, Vietnam was a unified country again, under the Communists. The U.S. Democratic Congress had cut funding in support of the South Vietnamese, and this contributed significantly to the downfall of the South.

Situation Analysis:

Both President Eisenhower and President Kennedy were hesitant about getting involved in a land war in Asia. However, they had to politically fight the domino theory that was prevalent since the 1940s, and it actually continued into the 1980s. This idea was that when one nation fell to Communism, another one would follow, soon thereafter. Around the globe, after World War Two, there were communist governments and insurrections taking place in many countries, supported by the USSR. Hungary, Poland, Czechoslovakia, China, North Korea, Malaya, Vietnam, Burma and Cambodia came under Communist insurrections and, in most cases, succumbed to this theory.

Vietnam was just one case of the communist disease. The feeling was that if the entire country fell into the Communist sphere, Thailand, Laos and Cambodia would probably follow. The Gulf of Tonkin incident was an excuse that the Johnson administration was looking for, to justify military action. However, there were two major missing strategies. There was no declaration of war and no strategy to obtain victory. The other major problem was that "mission creep" was used to send our military forces into Vietnam. If Johnson wanted to win, he should have asked Congress for a declaration of war and then sent in overwhelming forces to do the job. Since he was not willing to do this, he should not have entered the war at all.

For those readers who are not aware of the term "mission creep", it refers to the policy of sending in advisors, then a few combat troops, then more combat troops all over a period of time, almost ad infinitum. The result is that conditions on the battlefield always seem to require more troops. Vietnam is referred to as the granddaddy of mission creeps, since Kennedy sent in a few advisors and Johnson ended up with roughly 500,000 men in the country, over a period of four to five years.

This was a major **BLUNDER** on President Johnson's part. If he had asked for and obtained a declaration of war, he could have had Jane Fonda arrested and tried for treason. He should have allowed the generals in the field to plan and execute winning strategies, instead of micromanaging the war from Washington. If Washington had run World War Two, we probably would not have won that war. The Battle of the Bulge would have certainly turned out differently.

President Johnson got bogged down in a large Asian land war that was almost impossible to win. The Truman administration had blundered by not stopping the Communist Chinese from taking over China (see chapter four), and the Chinese now supported the North Vietnamese, with arms and military assistance. To win, it would have required the will to win and see it through. Overwhelming land forces would have been required. Bombing alone, while useful, does not win a war, unless one is willing to use atomic weapons. Nazi Germany was conquered by boots on the ground, not by strategic bombing. Japan was defeated by atomic weapons. Invasion of that country by ground forces would have been very costly, in human life.

The assassination of Ngo Dinh Diem, approved by the U.S., was another major **BLUNDER** by the Kennedy administration, since it set in motion a power play by the various military leaders in South Vietnamese. This led to chaos for some time in the South. The U.S. quietly approved the plan by the generals for the coup, because Ngo Dinh Diem was viewed as an impediment to U.S. aims in Southeast Asia. In addition, he seemed to have alienated most of the South Vietnamese people by acting like a dictator. As stated earlier in this chapter, the North Vietnamese leader, Ho Chi Minh, was delighted when he heard the news of the assassination.

The whole issue of the Tonkin Gulf Resolution, and the undeclared war, left many Americans with a lack of faith in the U.S. Government, and politicians in general. Inflation increased rapidly in the 1970s, and a malaise set in, within the entire United States. We had fought a "war" and the troops came home to no hero's welcome, as they had received at the end of World War Two. In fact, in many areas of the country, the population looked down on the returning veterans.

Two other major issues arose during the Vietnam era. First, the draft was seen as unfair, as many potential draftees received a deferment by either going to college or being married, with children. Thus, it seemed to the average person that most draftees, called up and sent to Vietnam, were single young men, from poor and lower income families. They could not afford to go to college and thus obtain a deferment. Second, there was the matter of "Guns" and "Butter". President Johnson figured he had two years to pass the Great Society programs, and therefore he did not want a war resolution from Congress. A declaration of war would have necessitated the use of federal dollars for the war effort ("guns"), and thus Congress would not have passed his Great Society ("butter") program.

First, America fought the Korean "War" (police action) in the 1950s and now, in the 1960s-1970s, we fought an undeclared war that ended with no victory. The North Vietnamese demonstrated, to the world at large, that they could and had defeated the super power, called the United States of America.

10

Czechoslovakia – Prague Spring
1968 - 1969

The country of Czechoslovakia arose out of the ashes of World War One. Before the Great War, the Kingdom of Bohemia was a province of the Austrian Empire, along with the areas named Moravia, Silesia, Upper Hungary and Carpathian Ruthenia. On the 28th of October 1918, Czechoslovakia declared its independence from the Austrian Empire. It was made up of the Czech lands (Bohemia/Moravia/Silesia) and Slovakia (Upper Hungary/Carpathian Ruthenia). As a country it survived for twenty years, until September 1938, when at the Munich conference between Germany, Britain, Italy and France, the Sudetenland (see chapter three) was ceded to Germany. Six months later, the Germans took over the rest of the country.

After World War Two, the Russian army occupied Czechoslovakia and formed a coalition government that did not last very long. By the 25th of February 1948 (Victorious February), the Communists had taken hold of the government and the entire country. On the 10th of March 1948, Jan Masaryk, an anti-

Communist and Czech patriot for years, was found dead in a courtyard below his bathroom window, dressed only in his pajamas. The police, most of whom were Communists, declared it was a suicide. Many Czechs believed that he had been murdered, and years later, after the fall of the Berlin Wall, details came out that he had, in fact, been pushed out of the window. Three months later, on the 7th of June 1948, the President of Czechoslovakia, Edvard Benes, resigned because he refused to sign the new communist constitution. The Communists were now in complete control of the country.

The first communist leader was Klement Gottwald (1948-1953), followed by Antonín Zápotocký (1953-1957). Finally, when Antonín Zápotocký died in 1957, Antonín Novotný became the leader of Czechoslovakia. Novotný remained the General Secretary of the Czech Communist Party, until 1968.

Fifteen years after the Berlin uprising and ten years after the Hungarian revolution, Czechoslovakia was struggling economically and Novotoný was blamed, by many in the party, for his economic policies. Alexander Dubček, a long time member of the Communist party, replaced Novotný as Communist party leader, on the 5th of January 1968. Novotný remained as the President of Czechoslovakia.

In February 1968, the party leadership, under Dubček, approved reform programs, in order to try and get the economy growing. Many intellectuals expressed the need for a repeal of the Press Censorship laws, and in March, the public demonstrated in support of the Dubček reforms and against President Novotný. By the 22nd of March 1968, Antonín Novotný resigned as President of Czechoslovakia and was replaced by a General Ludvík Svoboda, on March 30th. Svoboda had been a Czech patriot and a hero of the 1918 Russian civil war.

On the 5th of April 1968, the Czech communist party issued an Action Program that called for liberalization, over a ten year period. On the 18th of April, Alexander Dubček and Oldřich Černík formed a new government that pushed for a government with a "human face" and a democratization of the Czechoslovakian economic and political system. On the 1st of May, huge rallies supported the new programs, and Moscow started to become worried.

The Czech reformers traveled to Moscow and held a two day meeting (May 4th – 5th), with the Kremlin leadership, to explain the new programs and why they were necessary. The Kremlin was not convinced that this would turn out well, as far as communism was concerned, and Leonid Brezhnev started to consider the need for armed intervention. On the 29th of May, several Soviet generals visited the country, in order to plan some military exercises.

On the 26th of June 1968, censorship was abolished throughout Czechoslovakia. On the very next day, the reformers got together and issued a manifesto, calling for the democratization of the country. This was considered more radical, than the Dubček reform package. A week later, the Soviet army conducted the planned military exercises in Šumava, an area close to the German border, in order to place maximum pressure on the Czech Government.

TWILIGHT FOR THE WEST?

Timeline of Events Involving Czechoslovakia

DATES	EVENTS
28 October 1918	Czechoslovakia (Bohemia Kingdom) gained its independence
1 October 1938	German troops marched into Sudetenland, after deal between Hitler and Chamberlain
15 March 1939	Germany marched in and took over the entire country of Czechoslovakia
1 September 1939	World War II started after German troops invaded Poland
8 May 1945	World War Two in Europe officially ended upon the German surrender
9 May 1945	Russian troops entered Prague after defeating Germany
29 June 1945	Carpatho-Rus ceded to the Soviet Union by the Czechoslovakian government
25 February1948	Communists took over the government of Czechoslovakia, under Stalin's "Guidance"
1948 to 1953	Clement Gottwald became first leader of Communist Czechoslovakia
1953 to 1968	Communists, under Antonín Novotoný, ran the country under the "eye" of USSR
5 January 1968	Alexander Dubček became First Secretary of the Communist Party
5 April 1968	Alexander Dubček started a program of reforms, known as the "Prague Spring"
20 August 1968	Warsaw Pact forces rolled into Czechoslovakia and took over the country
20 August 1968	Dubček and supporters were flown to Moscow for talks with the USSR government
27 August 1968	Dubček and supporters returned to Prague from the Moscow talks
17 April 1969	Dubček forced to resign his position, and Gustáv Husák took over as First Secretary
1969 to 1989	The Communists under Gustáv Husák ran Czechoslovakia, for the next twenty years
29 December 1989	Václav Havel became president after the "Velvet" revolution forced Communists out
1 January 1993	Czechoslovakia split into two countries – the Czech Republic and Slovakia

In the middle of July, representatives of the Warsaw pact, excluding Czechoslovakia, met in Warsaw, Poland. They developed a sharply worded communiqué that stated the Czechoslovakia situation threatened all the socialist countries. At the end of the month, the Soviets and Czechs met to discuss the reforms, and the Czechs left with the threat of an invasion, by the Warsaw pact. At the same time, the Warsaw pact countries, except Czechoslovakia, held military exercises near the Czech border.

On the 3rd of August, a Warsaw pact meeting was held in Bratislava, a city located in Slovakia, the eastern region of Czechoslovakia. At this meeting, the Brezhnev doctrine of limited sovereignty was issued, for the first time. Basically, the doctrine stated that the threat to any one country in the Warsaw pact was a threat to all of them. A group of Czechoslovakian hard line Communists sent a note to Brezhnev, requesting that the Soviets intervene militarily.

On the 18th of August 1968, the Soviets decided that they must intervene militarily, in order to save communism and the other East European countries. Ultimately, on the 20th of August 1968, Czechoslovakia was invaded by 500,000 troops of the Warsaw pact. On the 21st of August at 3:00 am, the four leading reformers of Czechoslovakia, including Dubček, were arrested. President Svoboda called for calm and asked the people to go about their normal work. After the fighting was all over, seventy-two Czechoslovakian citizens had lost their lives, and thirteen officers and men of the Soviet Union military had been killed. The Soviet Union, however, had won, and the Brezhnev Doctrine was alive and well.

Dubček and the other reformers were flown to Moscow, where they were forced to sign a document, renouncing major parts of the reform package, and agreeing that Soviet forces could be stationed in the country. By the end of the month, censorship was re-imposed in the country, and the reformers had canceled the major parts of their reforms.

On the 28th of October 1968, Czechoslovakia became a federal republic, but it also reverted back to basically being a Communist, one party state. On the 17th of April 1969, Alexander Dubček was removed as the first secretary of the Czech Communist party. The removal of Dubcek, as party leader, was carried out under the orders of Leonid Brezhnev. The Soviet leader became upset when the Czech ice hockey team beat the Soviet team in the March, 1969 World Ice Hockey Championships in Stockholm, Sweden. After this USSR defeat, the citizens of Prague demonstrated in favor of their team and against the Soviet military. The disturbances, against the Soviet Union, irked the Soviet leader. Dubček was replaced by Gustáv Husák, as party leader, but he became the Speaker of the Federal Assembly, after being reelected to the seat he had held for years.

Later in 1969, he was appointed as Czech Ambassador to Turkey, hoping he would defect to the West. However, Dubček didn't defect, as Gustáv Husák had hoped, and he returned to Czechoslovakia in 1970, where he was expelled from the Communist

Party. He then returned to his former home and worked for the Forest Service, in Slovakia.

When the Berlin Wall came down and the Czech "Velvet Revolution" took place in 1989, Dubček was rehabilitated and became a national hero. The "Velvet Revolution" was the name given to a movement that was a non-violent transition of power in Czechoslovakia. It occurred during the last two months of 1989, and it was led by Vaclav Havel, who went on to become the President of the country. Dubček was elected Chairman of the Federal Assembly in 1989, 1990 and 1992, and he died in a car crash on the 7th of November 1992.

Although Dubček was always a Communist and had faith in communism, he believed in creating a socialist state with a "human face". This meant redefining the role of the Communist Party, and having the citizens firmly believe that communism/socialism, with some reforms, would provide an ideal life for them.

Situation Analysis:

The Prague Spring commenced fifteen years after the East German revolt and twelve years after the Hungarian revolution. In those two instances of revolt against communism, America and the West were missing in action. Radio Free Europe had encouraged the people suffering under the Soviet yoke to rise up, but the leaders of the West did nothing to help. Some were afraid of starting World War Three, but the question has never been asked, "Weren't the Soviets also afraid of starting a war, they could not win?"

The Eisenhower administration did nothing to help the East Germans, when they revolted against their Soviet masters. Three years later, the Eisenhower administration was given another chance to show some backbone, when the Hungarian revolted against their Soviet overlords. Again, America and the West did not help the Hungarians, in their desire for freedom. Radio Free Europe did not help matters by broadcasting support for the Hungarian cause.

When the Berlin Wall was built, the West was missing in action again. The Soviet troops and East Germans had been given orders not to resist, if the West knocked down the Wall in the first forty-eight hours. The West did nothing, except to broadcast how nasty the Soviets were. Words do not speak louder than actions.

In 1968, the West had another chance to recover their backbone, but **BLUNDERED** again. President Johnson was so tied up, in his Vietnam undeclared war, that he did not support the cries of help from Czechoslovakia. American tanks and forces were just across the border in Germany, but they did nothing.

The Johnson administration had eight months after the first stirrings of freedom in Czechoslovakia, but it did nothing. For these eight long months (January to August 1968), the West had the opportunity to provide moral support, and even military help, to the Czechs who wanted nothing, but freedom to run their country, as they saw fit. Radio Free Europe broadcast support for the Czechs crying for freedom, but the real support, they needed, never came. BY doing nothing, the Johnson Administration **APPEASED** the dictators in the Soviet Union, such as the rigid conservative Leonid Brezhnev and the more liberal Alexei Kosygin.

The Soviet Union, and its Eastern European allies, invaded the country with such overwhelming strength (an estimated 500,000 strong force) that the Czechs did not stand a chance. Obviously, the Soviets had read the "book" on how to invade a country with overwhelming force, take over (win) quickly and then withdraw most of your forces for another day. Carl von Clausewitz had been a prolific writer on the art of war, but President Johnson had obviously not read Clausewitz's theories, when he sent American troops into Vietnam, using the "mission creep" strategy. Obviously, he had read very few history books about waging war.

Force concentration is the practice of concentrating your forces, so as to bear an overwhelming presence on your enemy. The difference between the two sides then acts as a force multiplier, to the advantage of the superior forces.

By the time President Nixon took office in January 1969, the events in Czechoslovakia were basically over. The Soviets were in complete control, and Brezhnev had maintained his doctrine. It would be another twenty years, before President Reagan helped bring down the Berlin Wall, and the Czechs regained their freedom. In the meantime, Gustáv Husák ran the country in the typical communist way, with an iron fist.

11

Iran
1979 Islamic Revolution

The Qajar dynasty was the ruling power in Persia (Iran) from 1785 to 1925. Ahmad Shah Qajar was officially deposed in October 1925, and Reza Khan became Reza Shah Pahlavi. The major reason the Qajar dynasty collapsed was the occupation of Persia by the British, Russian and Turkish (Ottoman Empire) troops, during World War One.

Rezā Shāh ruled Persia (Iran) from 1925 until 1941. In 1935, Rezā Shāh requested that the West start using the name Iran, when referring to Persia. Since then, the country has, in most instances, been referred to as Iran, in the press and government documents. During his reign, he introduced many economic, political and social reforms that helped the common people, but annoyed the clergy. For example, women were encouraged to attend school and be educated. He basically laid the foundation of a modern state and tried to bring it up to Western standards. The Shah tried to de-emphasize the reliance on British assistance and turned to the Russians for help in improving his country.

103

Rezā Shāh accomplished many achievements during his reign, such as getting rid of malaria, creating the University of Iran, eliminating corruption amongst government officials, creating a national bank and building a major railroad. Of course, these modernizations of the country did not sit well with the conservative religious leaders.

This worked out fairly well for Iran, until World War Two. In August 1941, Britain and the Soviet Union invaded Iran, in order to protect the resources of the country and keep them out of German hands. Rezā Shāh was personally humiliated by this invasion, and the British gave him an out. He could resign, in favor of his son Mohammad Reza Pahlavi, and go into exile. This he did and, on the 16th of September 1941, he left Iran and went into exile, first in Mauritius and then on to South Africa, where he died three years later. His son Mohammad became the Shah on the same day, and he ruled Iran for approximately thirty-eight years.

Mohammad Reza Shah Pahlavi continued many of the improvements to Iranian institutions, after the end of World War Two. However, in the early 1950s, Iran went through a period of political upheaval, starting with the assassination, on the 7th of March 1951, of Ali Razmara, who was the Prime Minister. His assassination stemmed from the fact that he was not in favor of nationalizing the Anglo-Iranian Oil Company (AIOC), This Company was a joint venture between Great Britain and Iran, and it had developed the oil industry in Iran, since the early 1900s.

TWILIGHT FOR THE WEST?
Timeline of Events in Modern Day Iran

DATES	EVENTS
21 February 1921	Qajar Dynasty overthrown in a coup by the army under Reza Khan
15 December 1925	Reza Khan became the Shah of Iran and was known as Reza Shah Pahlavi
16 September 1941	Anglo Soviet invasion of Iran forced the abdication of Reza Shah Pahlavi
16 September 1941	Upon Reza Shah Pahlavi's abdication, Mohammad Reza Pahlavi became the Shah
28 April 1951	Mohammad Mosaddegh elected Prime Minister and nationalized the oil industry
19 August 1953	Coup d'état overthrew Mosaddegh, with CIA help and he was put on trial
16 January 1979	The Shah and his wife flew into exile, initially ended up in Egypt
1 February 1979	Ayatollah Khomeini returned to Tehran, from fourteen years of exile in Paris, France
4 November 1979	Militants took over the U.S. Embassy in Tehran and held 52 Americans hostage
3 December 1979	Ayatollah Khomeini became the Supreme Leader of Iran
22 September 1980	Iraq invaded Iran and started an eight year religious war; Sunnis versus Shiites
20 January 1981	The hostages released on the same day, as when President Reagan was sworn into office
20 August 1988	The Iran-Iraq war officially ended with Iran accepting the UN ceasefire proposal
3 June 1989	Ayatollah Khomeini, the Supreme Leader of Iran died of a heart attack
4 June 1989	Ayatollah Ali Khamenei became the Supreme Leader of Iran
8 July 1999	Students at Tehran University demonstrated against Salaam newspaper closure
27 June 2007	Protests erupted throughout Iran, after government imposed fuel rationing
June 2008 - 2009	US and Israel worked on the Stuxnet virus, used in cyber attack against nuclear site
13 June 2009	The Green Movement mounted a serious challenge to the theocracy, but put down

Mohammad
Reza Shah
Pahlavi

Razmara was replaced by Mohammad Mosaddegh of the National Front, and he was more or less an avowed communist. Mosaddegh nationalized the oil industry, five days after the assassination, and expelled the AIOC. This created great consternation in the West that needed Iranian oil, and they did not want to see Iran become a Soviet satellite. The British established an embargo on Iranian oil, and they blockaded any oil shipments out of the country.

For two years, this crisis played out and in August 1953, the Shah fled Iran. By then, the British had seen enough of the instability, and the British SIS, together with the American CIA, engineered a coup d'état. Codenamed, Operation Ajax, this coup resulted in the overthrow of the Mosaddegh government, and he was replaced as Prime Minister by a General Zahedi. The Shah returned from exile in Rome on the 23rd of August 1953 and, from then on, remained the ruling monarch, until the revolution in 1979.

TWILIGHT FOR THE WEST?

Mohammad Mosaddegh was put on trial and, on the 21st of December 1953, he was sentenced to three years of solitary confinement. After that he was placed under house arrest, until his death on the 5th of March 1967. To some Iranians, he was and still is considered a hero.

The years between 1954 and 1963 were fairly peaceful in Iran. The oil industry provided funds to help develop the country, and it increasingly became westernized, which again annoyed the conservative religious leaders.

Starting in January 1963, the Shah started on a program that increased this westernization of the country. Called the "White Revolution", the Shah wanted Iran to become a western style country where women had rights, reformation of the land and a western type, economic system. Many of these ideas came from his father. However, the conservatives in the country, urged on by the religious leaders, fought increasingly against these reforms. The Shah resorted to repressive measures, including the use of a secret police called SAVAK, to control the opposition to his policies.

The Shah also modernized the country's armed forces, and Iran became a bulwark of "freedom" against the USSR. On the 20th of January 1977, James Earl "Jimmy" Carter, Jr. became President of the United States and this changed the relationship between the USA and Iran that had existed for twenty-five years.

President Carter came into office having campaigned on several issues, including human rights.

Initially, he carried on his predecessors' program of supporting the Shah and his attempts to modernize Iran. During the month of October 1977, there were many demonstrations conducted against the Shah and his policies. Most of them were led by radical clerics that whipped up the religious zealots of the country.

United States of America President Jimmy Carter

From the 31st of December 1977 to the 1st of January 1978, President Carter visited Iran and he was hosted by the Shah with a state dinner. At the dinner, the Shah and President Carter gave traditional speeches. However, in the U.S. President's speech, Carter stated, "Iran, because of the great leadership of the Shah, is an island of stability in one of the more troubled areas of the world. This is a great tribute to you, Your Majesty, and to your leadership and to the respect and admiration and love which your people give to you."

Right after Carter and his party left Iran, demonstrations and riots against the Shah intensified. In the later part of 1978, there were strikes and demonstrations that basically paralyzed the country. All the while, President Carter and his administration were pressuring the Shah to release political prisoners, religious fundamentalists and communists in the name of human rights. "Human Rights" was the campaign slogan of Carter and it was based on his religious beliefs, backed by his Baptist background.

The British Labour government and the Carter administration also withheld funds from both the Shah's government and the religious leaders in Iran. As 1978 progressed, the Shah was under increasing pressure, from the religious groups in Iran and from the American government. The Carter administration withheld shipments of arms, in an effort to persuade the Shah to change course. Even, members of the Carter government disagreed amongst themselves, as to the best approach in changing the direction of Iran.

In early 1979, everything came to a head. Just one year after Carter had claimed that Iran, under the Shah, was an island of stability, the Shah was basically thrown under the proverbial bus by President Jimmy Carter. On the 16th of January 1979, the Shah left Iran for exile in Egypt, leaving Shahpur Bakhtiar in charge of Iran, as Prime Minister. On the 1st of February, Ayatollah Khomeini returned to Iran from his exile in Paris, France, and he received a hero's welcome at Tehran airport.

Ayatollah Khomeini
Supreme Leader of
Islamic Iran until he
died 3rd of June 1989

On the 11th of February 1979, the rebel Iranians, supported by the religious leaders, defeated the Shah's loyal troops, and, on the 1st of April, a referendum was held, to get approval for the establishment of an Islamic Republic and approval for a new theocratic-republican constitution. Both were supposedly approved by the voters, and by December 1979, Khomeini became supreme leader of Iran.

On the 4th of November 1979, Iranian students invaded and seized the American Embassy in Tehran, taking the staff captive. In all, fifty-two American diplomats were held hostage for 444 days, until their release on the 20th of January 1981, the day of Ronald Reagan's inauguration as President. An attempt to rescue them in April 1980 ended in disaster, when a dust storm forced some of the helicopters to land. One helicopter actually hit a plane in the Iranian desert operation base.

The year 1980 saw major changes in Iran. There were mass imprisonments and executions of the Shahs' supporters, teachers were fired, and Iran turned into a country that was much worse than it ever was under the Shah. Khomeini had written and spoken about how he would run Iran, if given the chance, but very few Iranians actually found out about this, until it was too late. On the 22nd of September 1980, Iraq invaded Iran, and the ensuing war lasted until 1988. The war resembled the Great War in Europe, almost seventy years before, in that trenches were built everywhere, and the slaughter on both sides was surreal. It was basically a war between the

Sunnis and the Shea, somewhat like the Protestants and Catholics in Europe, five hundred years before.

Situation Analysis:

President James Earl Carter, and his administration, committed a **massive BLUNDER** when they threw the Shah under the proverbial bus. Under President Carter, the Secretary of State was Cyrus Vance and Zbigniew Brzezinski was the National Security Advisor to the President. Vance and Brzezinski clashed frequently over the approach to take on Iran. To Brzezinski's credit, he saw the approaching dangers in throwing the Shah under the bus and allowing Khomeini to return to Iran.

The Eisenhower, Johnson, Nixon and Ford administrations all supported the Shah strongly. He was pro-American and anti-USSR, which made him a valuable supporter in the rivalry between the USA and the Soviets. Meanwhile, in 1961, Khomeini had an opportunity to take over the leadership of the Iranian Shia clergy on the death of Ayatollah Sayyed Husayn Borujerdi. Khomeini became a "thorn" in the side of the Shah at every turn. He opposed the Shah's "White Revolution" because he saw the program as a westernization of Iran. The people would turn again to the conservative Islamic faith, if they became too westernized.

In the early 1970s, Khomeini had given lectures about the virtues of an Islamic government, and he even wrote some books on the subject. These lectures and books extolled the virtues of Sharia law, and the requirement to stamp out non-Islamic influences from the West. These ideas, of religious leaders governing Iran, were publicized only to the known opposition of the Shah. Khomeini didn't want to alarm the Western powers, until it was too late.

Western intelligence agents failed to spot these ideas being spoken and written about. If they did, they were not reported to the leaders of the West, especially America. In 1977, Ali Shariati, who had popularized the idea of an Islamic revival in Iran, died, and Khomeini finally was the leading opposition to the Shah.

Again, the Carter administration did not see all this happening, except for maybe Brzezinski. Jimmy Carter continued on his human rights campaign and, at every turn, pushed the Shah to release prisoners and stop torturing political and religious leaders. Carter was naïve in his thinking and believed any religious leader had to be good, like the Pope, the Archbishop of Canterbury or his Baptist ministers. He made a major **BLUNDER** and did not foresee that the conservative Islamic leaders might be worse than the Shah.

As Carter persuaded the Shah to liberalize more and more, so Khomeini's power and influence grew. Even Carter's UN ambassador Andrew Young was fooled, and he thought that Khomeini might even become a saint and a hero. Carter believed in human rights, but where was he, when Khomeini took over in the fall of 1979 and started to execute the opposition. Carter learned firsthand his **BLUNDER** when the students seized the US embassy and held the diplomats hostage for 444 days.

The French president at the time, Giscard d'Estaing, was appalled, when he came to realize that Carter was throwing, under the bus, its strongest ally in the Middle East, in favor of a Muslim Islamic extremist. Iran went on to be placed on the U.S. State Department list of State Sponsors for International Terrorism. Since the takeover of Iran by Khomeini and his religious zealots, the country has supported Hezbollah and Hamas with funds and arms. As long as the Mullahs run Iran, there will be no freedom for the Iranians, and no peace in the Middle East.

Carter's **BLUNDER** of 1978 has led to thirty-five years of death and chaos throughout the Middle East, with no end in sight. (Chapter twenty covers Iran's objective of obtaining a nuclear weapon).

12

Iraq
1990 - 1991, 2003 – 2011

At the end of World War One, in which the Ottoman Empire collapsed, Iraq became a League of Nations Mandate. Some British and French bureaucrats drew boundaries and created countries, as the Turks retreated. Iraq became a mandate of the League on the 11th of November 1920, and Britain was given the task of running the country. In order to help them run the country, Britain installed Faisal I as the King of Iraq. Faisal was a Hashemite, and the Sunnis, who were a minority in Iraq, were appointed to key government positions, to help him rule.

In 1932, Britain granted independence to the Iraq kingdom, at the request of King Faisal, but the British were permitted to maintain military bases in the country. When King Faisal I died in 1933, King Ghazi took over and ruled Iraq until 1939, when he died. King Ghazi was succeeded by his son Faisal II, who was not of age, and a regent, Abd al-Ilah, ruled in his place, until Faisal was old enough to rule himself.

TWILIGHT FOR THE WEST?

Timeline of Events in Modern Day Iraq up to 2006

DATES	EVENTS
11 November 1920	League of Nations created Iraq and gave the British authority to operate it
3 October 1932	Britain granted Iraq independence and King Faisal I was installed
4 April 1939	King Feisal II became king of Iraq on his father's death
14 July 1958	The monarchy was overthrown by the military and Faisal was shot
16 July 1979	Saddam Hussein became president after Al-Bakr resigned, at least 20 rivals shot
22 September 1980	Iraq invaded Iran and started an eight year religious war; Sunnis versus Shiites
7 June1981	Israel bombed the Iraq nuclear plant near Bagdad in Operation Opera
20 August 1988	The Iran Iraq war officially ended with Iran accepting the UN cease fire proposal
2 August 1990	Iraq invaded Kuwait and took over the oil fields to help pay for Iraq-Iran war
6 August 1990	President George H.W.Bush started assembly of 500,000 troops from various nations
17 January 1991	Operation Desert Storm commenced with the bombing of Iraq facilities
27 February 1991	Kuwait was freed but not before the Iraqis left and set fire to the oil fields
19 March 2003	President George W Bush commenced a military campaign to oust Saddam Hussein
1 May 2003	Major military operations ended in Iraq and Saddam Hussein went into hiding
1 May 2003	Almost immediately an insurgency arose and US found itself in a guerilla war in the towns
13 December 2003	Saddam Hussein was found hiding in a hole in a farm near the town of Tikrit
30 January 2005	The first free election in fifty years was held in Iraq with high turnout
19 October 2005	Saddam Hussein went on trial in an Iraqi court and eventually sentenced to death
30 December 2006	Ex president Saddam Hussein was executed by the Iraqi government

115

On the 1st of April 1941, during World War Two, there was a coup d'état by members of a group called the Golden Square. A month later, the British invaded Iraq, in order to secure the oil supplies, and to prevent the Germans from getting access to them. The British occupied Iraq until 1947, when the Hashemite monarchy was restored.

King Faisal II ruled Iraq until 1958 when, on the 14th of July, there was another coup d'état, led by the army and a Brigadier General Abd al-Karim Qasim. The monarchy was overthrown, and King Faisal was shot, in order to discourage any attempt, by the royalists, to bring the monarchy back. General Qasim ruled Iraq for five years until 1963, when he was overthrown by another coup d'état. For the next five years, there was turmoil in Iraq and a couple more coups d'état. In 1968, the Ba'ath party, under Ahmed Hassan al-Bakr, took over, and a General Saddam Hussein, who was vice president, slowly gained more and more power.

Saddam Hussein
President of Iraq
1979 to 2003

On the 16th of July 1979, President Ahmed Hassan al-Bakr resigned for health reasons and Saddam Hussein assumed the presidency. Saddam Hussein, like President Jimmy Carter, naively welcomed the overthrow of the Shah in Iran, but when Khomeini called for the expansion of Islamic ideas into Iraq, with its Shia majority, Hussein saw the error of his ways. A year after he became the President of Iraq, Hussein declared war against Iran, on the 22nd of September 1980,. The war lasted for eight, long years, and it resembled the trench warfare of the Great War. The death toll was high, and no accurate figure has ever become available. Probably, each side lost a minimum of 100,000 each and maybe up to 500,000.

While this war was going on, Israel attacked and destroyed the Iraqi nuclear reactor at Osirak on the 7th of June 1981. It was of the French Osiris class design, and Iraq claimed it was for peaceful purposes, although the Israelis believed otherwise.

On the 2nd of August 1990, Iraq invaded Kuwait, claiming it was the 19th province of Iraq. After the expensive Iran-Iraq war of the 1980s, Saddam Hussein needed extra revenue to pay off the massive war debts, and Kuwait's oil industry was a tempting target. Hussein alleged that Kuwait had always been part of Iraq, and it was right that it should be absorbed into the country.

Three days after the Iraq invasion of Kuwait, President George H.W. Bush drew a line in the sand and stated that the invasion would not stand. The next day, plans were drawn up to move up to 500,000 U.S. combat men from around the world, including required equipment/weapon systems, to Saudi Arabia, for the purpose of driving the Iraqis out of Kuwait. Over the next few months, these men and heavy equipment flowed into the Saudi Kingdom that was also afraid of an invasion by Hussein.

George H. W. Bush
41st U.S. President
1989 to 1993

General Norman Schwarzkopf (nicknamed Storming Norman) was assigned the task to send the Iraqis packing from Kuwait. This mission was designated Operation Desert Storm. The ultimate force, for Operation Desert Storm, consisted of 500,000 US personnel, plus 250,000 personnel from other nations who had signed up for the cause. From August 1990 to January 1991, Schwarzkopf planned the attack to drive Hussein's soldiers from Kuwait.

In November 1990, the UN Security Council approved "all means necessary" to drive Iraq out of Kuwait and, on the 17th of January 1991, the air attack on Iraq commenced, with attacks by Tomahawk missiles and stealth F-117s. The Iraqi command and control centers were severely damaged. For the next month, the air attacks continued in order to soften up Hussein's forces.

Finally, on the 24th of February, the ground attack commenced, and after four days of fighting, a cease-fire was agreed to, with the Iraqi forces withdrawing from Kuwait. The main road leading out of Kuwait towards Iraq, officially named highway 80 and nicknamed "the highway of death", became a slaughter house, with over five hundred Iraqi vehicles of all types being destroyed. On the 8th of June 1981, a victory parade by the U.S. military took place in Washington.

The United States did not advance on Baghdad, and President George H. W. Bush left the Iraqi dictator Hussein in control. This issue will be discussed in the Situation Analysis at the end of this chapter.

For the next twelve years, Saddam Hussein (a Sunni) remained in firm control of Iraq and his regime carried out massacres of the Shiite majority, mainly in the south of Iraq.

George W. Bush
43rd U. S President
2001 to 2009

Two years after the New York twin towers were brought down by Islamic terrorists flying planes into them on the 11th of September 2001, President George W. Bush decided the U.S. had to invade Iraq, in order to eliminate their WMD (Weapons of Mass Destruction) program. After 9/11, the U.S. pressured Iraq to allow nuclear inspectors into the country, but Hussein resisted at every turn, raising the suspicion that he was hiding something.

Operation Iraqi Freedom, sometimes known as the second Iraq War, started on the 20th of March 2003, with the involvement of a total of approximately 265,000 troops, including 148,000 from the United States. This was a third of the number involved in Operation Desert Storm (First Iraq War). This operation ended with the fall of Baghdad, on the 10th of April 2003. According to estimates, the U.S. casualties from this operation were 139 dead, and the British lost 33 dead, while the Iraqi casualties were 9,200 dead and 3,750 non-combatants were killed.

Saddam Hussein was captured on the 13th of December 2003, in a hole on a farm close to the town ad-Dawr, which was near Tikrit. With his capture, some people considered that the Iraq war was actually over, but this was far from fact. No weapons of mass destruction were ever discovered, and an insurrection commenced that lasted for several years. Some people consider that the insurgency is still continuing, and peace has never been achieved in Iraq. According to estimates, the United States suffered 4,491 soldiers killed, since the end of the war, and 47, 541 injured.

These casualties were mainly from suicide bombs and IEDs (improvised explosive devices).

The following chart developed by the U.S. Defense Department shows the troop levels and casualties by year.

U.S. troops in Iraq

President Barack Obama has ordered all U.S. troops out of Iraq by Dec. 31. Troop levels and deaths by month since the U.S. invasion in March

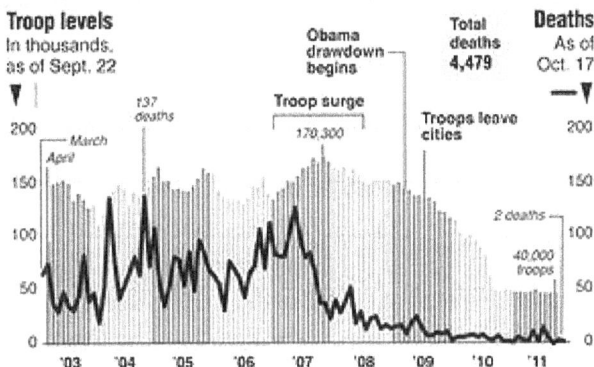

Source: Congressional Research Service, U.S. Defense Department, iCasualties
Graphic: Judy Treible

© 2011 MCT

Situation Analysis:

President George Herbert Walker Bush (no. 41), and his administration, did not commit any blunders in the conduct of events leading up to the first Iraq War, and the forced removal of Iraqi forces from Kuwait. The United States followed the ideas laid out by Carl von Clausewitz two hundred years before, by applying maximum strength right from the beginning of the operation. General Schwarzkopf made the right plans and carried them out effectively, using the 750,000 soldier strong army.

Some analysts who have studied this war believe that President Bush did **BLUNDER,** when he did not advance into Iraq proper and take out Saddam Hussein, while he had the overwhelming forces to do so. By leaving Hussein in place, Bush is partially to blame for the killing of thousands of Shiite Muslims in southern Iraq over the next twelve years, by the Republican guard and other Iraqi forces.

It is understood that Bush was concerned about the Arab troops, from Saudi Arabia, Syria and other Arab countries that might be offended, if the United States invaded an Arab country. Saddam Hussein was a Sunni Muslim, and most Saudis were also of the Sunni sect.

Overall, President George H. W. Bush conducted the war extremely well, except for the fact that he forgot that victory was the goal. Leaving Saddam Hussein in power meant that another war was going to have to take place, to remove the tyrant.

The 11th of September 2001 was a major turning point in the United States, as well as the Middle East. Most people in the United States realized that Islamic terrorists presented a major threat, even if some modern day Chamberlains were in denial. Right after the 9/11 event, the U.S., with help from other nations, went into Afghanistan to clear out the Al-Qaeda training camps. There was also concern mainly in the U.S. and Britain that Iraq was trying to amass WMDs and would threaten Europe and America.

Accordingly, President George W. Bush (no. 43) decided that America should invade Iraq, together with the British led by Tony Blair, in order to overthrow Hussein and prevent Iraq from acquiring WMDs. However, this is where a major **BLUNDER** occurred by George W. Bush. Obviously he had not studied history enough to realize one needs overwhelming force to win decisively.

The troop strength was sufficient enough to win the initial battle, but the Bush administration did not understand that they required additional troops to control the country. The U.S. disbanded the Iraqi army and most of the police, as soon as Baghdad fell. Since Iraq had a population of around thirty million, the U.S. needed probably double the troop strength to maintain order and prevent what happened; urban warfare.

Bush's Secretary of Defense, Donald Rumsfeld, totally misunderstood what would happen, when the Iraqi defense and police structure collapsed. The actual war only caused 139 deaths among the U.S. forces, but the urban warfare, after the war, caused 4,491 deaths. Most of these were from suicide bombs, ambushes or IEDs hidden under the roads

General David Petraeus recognized the problem and recommended a troop surge that took place in 2007. This helped correct the initial problem from the lack of a significant number of troops. Before President Bush left office, he was negotiating with the Iraqi government to allow the U.S. to stage troops in the country, for its protection and training of its security forces. The actual details of the pact were still being negotiated, when President Bush left office, and the new president, Barack Obama failed to consummate the deal with the result that it fell through.

The consequence, from the lack of a troop agreement, was that all American troops were withdrawn at the end of 2011, and Iraq started to fall into chaos. This is discussed in a future part of this book (chapter sixteen). The sad story about Iraq is that since 1920 the country has had very few years of real peaceful existence, without internal or external violence. **BLUNDER**, after **BLUNDER**, has occurred, and the country could ultimately be divided into three parts; Sunni, Shia and Kurds.

13

Georgia
2008

The country of Georgia, not to be confused with the U.S. State of Georgia, has a long history of independence and being invaded by Russia and other empires. It abuts on the Black Sea and is surrounded by Turkey, Russia, Armenia and Azerbaijan. After the Russian revolution of 1917, Georgia declared its independence from Russia, on the 26th of May 1918. It lasted less than three years, because in February 1921 the Red Army invaded Georgia, and it remained part of the USSR until the Berlin Wall and the Soviet Union collapsed, almost seventy years later.

On the 9th of April 1991, Georgia formally declared its independence from the Soviet Union, and it has remained more or less free, not withstanding some incursions by Russian troops. In 1992, Eduard Shevardnadze, the former Soviet Foreign Minister, was elected the second president of Georgia. He remained as president until 2003, when the Rose Revolution took place, and Mikheil Saakashvili was voted into the presidential office.

RICHARD OSBORN

While Shevardnadze was in office, Vladimir Putin became president of the Russian Federation in the year 2000, and he remained in office until the 7th of May 2008.   In 2008, Putin could not run again as president, so he supported Dmitry Medvedev for the presidency and he became Prime Minister.   Putin's ultimate goal is to try and put the USSR back together.

Regions of Georgia, mainly Ossetia and Abkhazia, were populated by people who were of Russian descent and were decidedly pro-Russian. From April 2008 until the end of August 2008, Georgia became a country in turmoil, as Putin took a page from Hitler's playbook (Sudetenland).   Pro-Russian separatists in Abkhazia and South Ossetia stirred up trouble, claiming they were being harassed by the Georgian government and its forces. This is what the German Nazi sympathizers did in the Sudetenland in 1938.

126

TWILIGHT FOR THE WEST?

Timeline of Events in Russian/Georgian 2008 Conflict

DATES	EVENTS
25 February 1921	Georgia became a Soviet Socialist Republic after being invaded by Russia
9 April 1991	Georgia declared its independence after the USSR collapsed
7 May 2000	Russian Vladimir Putin became President of Russia after Boris Yeltsin resigned
23 November 2003	Eduard Shevardnadze, pro-Russian Georgia president, resigned during Rose movement
25 January 2004	Mikheil Saakashvili became the third president of Georgia, was not pro-Russian
8 May 2008	Vladimir Putin became Prime Minister after serving eight years as President of Russia
1 August 2008	Ossetia separatists began shelling Georgian villages and intense fighting occurred
5 August 2008	Volunteers from North Ossetia started to arrive in South Ossetia
6 August 2008	Women and children were evacuated from South Ossetia
7 August 2008	Georgian President Saakashvili announced unilateral ceasefire. Fighting intensified
8 August 2008	Russians started to move troops into South Ossetia in support of the separatists
8 August 2008	Georgia launched an offensive to surround the capital of South Ossetia
9 August 2008	A Georgian missile boat was sunk by the Russian Navy after it entered Russian zone
9 August 2008	Second front opened in the war in Kodori Valley in separatist Abkhazia
11 August 2008	Russia ruled out peace talks until Georgia withdrew from South Ossetia
12 August 2008	French President Sarkozy negotiated a ceasefire that didn't solve the issues
14 August 2008	Polish President Kaczynski in Tbilisi declared today Georgia, tomorrow the Ukraine
16 August 2008	Russians occupied Georgia's bases of Poti, Goti and Senaki destroyed the military bases
19 August 2008	Georgian and Russian forces exchanged POWs
23 August 2008	Russia announced that it had withdrawn its forces into Abkhazia and South Ossetia

The problems between Russia and Georgia started on the 16th of April 2008, when President Putin of Russia signed a decree authorizing all government agencies to deal directly with Abkhazia and South Ossetia separatists. Georgia appealed to the United Nations to get Russia to negate this decree. Four days later, a Georgian drone flying over the Abkhazia on a reconnaissance mission was shot down, either by a Russian Mig-29 or a Su-27. On the 23rd of April, the U.N. Security Council held a meeting, and the result was that the four major Western powers called on Russia to revoke the decree.

Russia refused to repeal the authorization, and in early May it increased its troop strength (peacekeepers) in Abkhazia, by roughly 2,500. This was still under the upper limit, authorized in 1994 by the Commonwealth of Independent States. Georgian claimed that these peacekeepers were actually armed soldiers, with heavy military equipment. Russia denied the accusation. On the 31st of May 2008, Russia sent in more men ostensibly for the purpose of repairing a rail line in Abkhazia. Actually, this railway line would be extremely useful, if Russia decided to invade the main part of Georgia. This Russia did in August 2008, and the railway line was used to transport over 9,000 troops (see later in this chapter).

In the early part of July 2008, bombings and violence increased dramatically in South Ossetia. Violence extended to both pro-separatists and pro-Georgian government officials. On the 7th of July, some soldiers of the Georgian government were taken prisoner by South Ossetia separatists. Again, this was a page out of Hitler's 1938 playbook. On the 8th of July, four Russian Air Force jets flew over South Ossetia in a show of force.

In the middle of the month, two parallel military exercises were conducted, one by the United States and Georgia, and the other by the Russians. It was a "coincidence" they both happened at the same time. The Russian exercise included some training for "peacekeepers" that were scheduled to go to South Ossetia and Abkhazia.

By early August, all the problems and incursions came to a head, and the 2008 Russian-Georgian "war" commenced. On the 1st of August 2008, a Georgian government police vehicle was blown up by an improvised explosive device, and in retaliation, Georgia attacked South Ossetia border guards, killing four and wounding seven of them. On the same day Ossetian separatists, mainly from North Ossetia, began shelling villages in Georgia, with guns provided by Russia. Georgia and the separatists exchanged fire for three days, mainly under the cover of darkness.

Russia evacuated women and children of the pro-Russian separatists and took them to neighboring Russia and its North Ossetia region. Volunteers flowed into the South Ossetia region from Russia, and on the 6th of August, fighting commenced between the Georgian troops and the separatist forces.

On the 7th of August, Georgia moved heavy vehicles and artillery, towards the area of the fighting in South Ossetia. In the late afternoon of the 7th, the Georgian President announced a unilateral ceasefire, and it held for about three hours. At the end of the ceasefire, heavy fighting resumed along the entire front. Russia accused the Georgians of using the ceasefire to position heavy weapons on the frontline. That evening, Russia moved tanks into the South Ossetia region, and by midnight a full blown "war" started.

On the 8th of August, Russia committed army and airborne troops to the battle, and the fighting continued all of the day. The Russian Air Force became involved with sorties against Georgian troops, and a few aircraft were shot down by Georgian forces. By the end of the day, Russian troops were advancing along the entire front, and by the 9th of August, the Georgians were outnumbered by the Russian forces.

On the 10th of August, the Russians advanced into Georgia proper, and they seriously damaged the town of Gori, the birth place of Joseph Stalin, with bombs and artillery shells. By the 13th, Russian troops occupied Gori and cut the communications between the Georgian capital Tbilisi and the western regions of the country. Russia occupied the town for twelve days, before withdrawing on the 22nd of August.

Meanwhile at the same time, as the battle for South Ossetia was being waged, a battle in and around the region of Abkhazia commenced. On the 9th, the regions army and air force began attacking Georgian government forces, and on the 10th, the Russian navy started a blockade of the region's coast, sinking one approaching Georgian vessel. On the 11th of August, Russian paratroopers, stationed in Abkhazia, started to attack Georgian government forces.

As the war progressed, Russia destroyed six Georgian ships in the Poti harbor and took several Georgian soldiers prisoner. Tbilisi, the Georgian capital was bombed, including the main airport and the Tbilisi aircraft plant. All the while, that the war was being waged, both Georgia and Russia broadcast propaganda continuously over radio and television.

Finally, on the 12th of August, President Medvedev of Russia declared an end to Russia's "peace" operation in the country of Georgia, and specifically in South Ossetia and Abkhazia. On the same day, French President Sarkozy got approval, from Russia and Georgia, for his six point peace plan. Two days later, the presidents of South Ossetia and Abkhazia signed the agreement. On the 16th of August, Russia and Georgia signed the peace plan, officially ending the war between Russia and Georgia.

Before the treaty went into effect, Russia started to destroy Georgia military hardware, as much as they could. Even though, as of the 16th, the treaty was in effect, skirmishes continued between the two forces for a few days. By the 23rd of August, the bulk of Russian forces were withdrawn, across the border into the Russian Federation. Buffer zones were left in place in Abkhazia and South Ossetia, which were manned by Russian "peace keepers".

The 23rd of August 2008 is the day that the Russian-Georgian War ended, but with Putin in power as Prime Minister and then President again, it could start up again in the future. He still has that long held dream of reconstituting the Soviet Union which is discussed in chapter twenty-one of this book. In the

131

meantime Georgia, in effect, lost two of its regions; Abkhazia and South Ossetia.

Situation Analysis:

Vladimir Putin, ex KGB officer and acting Prime Minister under Boris Yeltsin, became President of the Russian Federation on the 7th of May 2000, after Yeltsin resigned. Ever since the Soviet Union collapsed in the early 1990s, Putin has dreamed of righting the historical wrongs of the disintegration of the USSR and putting it back together.

The disputes between Georgia and Russia over the South Ossetia and Abkhazia regions of Georgia dated back to 1992 and 1994 respectively. When the Soviet Union broke up into individual republics, like Georgia, and they declared their independence, there were disputes as to what should happen to the former USSR military bases. In addition, there were problems in the protection of the Russian minorities in these regions.

In South Ossetia, a three-part peacekeeping force was developed that consisted of Russian, Georgian and South Ossetia forces. The Agreement was signed on the 24th of June 1992, and it did not allow the Russian peacekeepers to move outside of the specified region.

Initially, after the USSR broke up, there was some ethnic cleansing carried on in Abkhazia, and Yeltsin issued a decree on the 9th of June 1994 that allowed for an operation to secure peace in the region. Further extension of the peacekeeping force decree was agreed to, and the Russian forces were allowed remain in the region, until full completion of the peacekeeping operation. There did not seem to be any definitive guidelines, as to when the goals of the operation would be declared completed.

The situation in both regions ended up to be ideal for President Putin and the Russians to instigate and cause trouble. Putin took a page out of Hitler's 1930s playbook. The difference between Putin and Hitler is that Putin is not in any hurry to put the Soviet Union back together. Putin used the idea of protecting Russian speaking people, in the contested regions, for justifying sending troops in, during 2008.

The problem was that the United States, under President Bush, was not willing to send troops in to protect Georgia or to send major arms to help them fight off the Russians. NATO did not offer any help either. This was a **BLUNDER,** because it taught Putin the West was not willing to go to war, over areas that used to be part of the USSR.

U.S. President
George W. Bush
with
Georgian President
Mikheil Saakashvili

Putin learned this lesson very well and decided he could continue on his plan to resurrect the USSR, when he took over Crimea and instigated trouble in the Ukraine (chapter twenty-one of this book).

As far as the Russian-Georgian War is concerned, there was also **APPEASEMENT** by President Nicolas

Sarkozy of France, who developed a ceasefire agreement recognizing the independence of South Ossetia and Abkhazia. Originally Sarkozy's plan had four points (1-4), but Russia objected and had two more points (5, 6) added.

1. The non-use of force
2. The definitive cessation of hostilities
3. Free access for humanitarian aid
4. The withdrawal of the Georgian military forces to their usual bases
5. The withdrawal of Russian military forces to the lines they held before hostilities broke out. While waiting for an international body, the Russian peacekeeping forces will implement additional security measures
6. The opening of international discussions on the modalities of security and stability in Abkhazia and South Ossetia.

Russian tanks were only thirty miles from Tbilisi, the capital of Georgia, and if they did not sign the pact, the Russians would soon be in the capital. President Saakashvili had no choice, but to sign the agreement, if he wanted to keep Georgia together.

Georgia is still in the crosshairs of Russia's Putin and his armed forces. Sarkozy's plan, which was an **APPEASEMENT**, did nothing to resolve the conflict, and the hostilities continued for a few more days. The status of the two regions is still in dispute, and Georgia has no control over them. A few countries, including Russia, have recognized the independence of the two regions.

14

Egypt
2011

Hosni Mubarak, a former air force officer, was vice president of Egypt, from 1975 to 1981, under President Anwar Al Sadat. On the 6th of October 1981, President Sadat was assassinated while reviewing a victory parade celebrating the 1973 Suez Canal crossing by Egypt. Islamic Jihadists carried out the attack on Sadat with grenades and bullets. Eight days after the assassination of Sadat, Mubarak became President of Egypt and served in that capacity for thirty years, until February 2011.

During the first twenty-eight years of Mubarak's presidency, events in Egypt were fairly peaceful, although a few disturbances occurred, as is normal in the Middle East. While Mubarak was President of Egypt, four U.S. Presidents, Ronald Reagan, George H.W. Bush, Bill Clinton and George W. Bush, worked with him, to maintain fairly peaceful cooperation between Egypt and Israel.

All this started to change with the speech by U.S. President Barack Obama at Cairo University on the 4th of June 2009. This speech has been dubbed "The

Apology Tour" by many Americans, because Obama apologized to the university students about how America in the past had acted arrogantly and imperially. Actually, it could have been called the Appeasement Tour, as the speech was pro-Arab and pro-Muslim, while being somewhat anti-American. It was obvious that President Obama was not pro Mubarak, even though he was speaking in Egypt. This speech, in all likelihood, gave encouragement to the anti-Mubarak crowd.

From 2009 to the beginning of 2011, unrest by college students started to increase and was controlled heavy handily by the Mubarak government. Also, during this time, the Muslim Brotherhood was gaining strength throughout the Egyptian population. The current leader of Al Qaeda, Dr. Ayman al-Zawahihi, was an Egyptian by birth and joined the Muslim Brotherhood, when he was only fourteen years old. In the twentieth century, the Muslim Brotherhood was outlawed many times, by different Egyptian governments, and was also labeled a terrorist organization.

The Arab Spring, as it became known, started in Tunisia, at the end of 2010, when a street vendor burned himself alive. In Egypt, it all started to come to a head on the 25th of January 2011, when Egyptians took to the streets on the "Day of Anger". On this day, protests erupted in cities throughout Egypt, and specifically there were protests against police brutality. The protesters demanded the resignation of the Minister of Interior, restoration of the minimum wage, term limits on the presidency and an end to the Egyptian emergency law.

For the next two days, the protests and riots continued unabated, with the Muslim Brotherhood declaring support for the demonstrations. Hundreds of rioters and protesters, including journalists and members of the Muslim Brotherhood, were arrested by the police.

On Friday the 28th of January 2011, labeled the "Friday of Anger", thousands of protesters filled the streets, shortly after prayers. The disturbances continued all day, with rioting and looting becoming the norm. Shots were fired and some protesters died. Government buildings were set on fire. Finally, the military joined the police in trying to stop the protests. The rioting did die down during the night, and the next two days saw fewer demonstrations.

Egyptian President Hosni Mubarak
1981 - 2011

Timeline of Events in Modern Day Egypt

DATES	EVENTS
1936 - 1952	King Farouk ruled Egypt for 16 years but he was a disliked monarch
1952-1953	Farouk was forced to abdicate in favor of his young son and a regency council rules
18 June 1953	General Muhammad Neguib deposed King Farouk's son and declared a republic
14 November 1954	Revolutionary Command Council lead by Colonel Nasser ousted and arrested Neguib
23 June 1956	Gamal Abdel Nasser officially became President of Egypt
26 July 1956	Nasser nationalized the Suez Canal and later England and France invaded the canal zone
5 June 1967	Six day war started between the Egypt, Syria and Israel
10 June 1967	Six day war ended with Israel camped on the Suez canal
28 September 1970	President Gamal Abdel Nasser died of a heart attack
15 October 1970	Vice President Anwar Sadat was sworn in as President
6 October 1973	Yom Kipper war was started by Egypt under Sadat against Israel
15 October 1973	Yom Kipper war ended with Israel no longer camped on the Suez Canal
26 March 1979	Peace Treaty between Egypt and Israel is signed with Israel leaving the Sinai
6 October 1981	Sadat is assassinated by fundamentalist officers at a military review
14 October 1981	Vice President Hosni Mubarak became President of Egypt and ruled almost 30 years
4 June 2011	US President Obama gave apology speech "A New Beginning" at Cairo University
25 January 2011	Mass protests started against Mubarak in Cairo and continued for 18 days
11 February 2011	President Mubarak suddenly resigned, even though he stated he would stay until Sept.
30 June 2012	Muhammad Morsi, of the Moslem Brotherhood, became President of Egypt
29 November 2014	President Mubarak is cleared from all charges, arising from deaths in Arab Spring

The 30th and 31st of January saw more rioting, looting and arson, which caused the government to set curfews, in most parts of the country. During the day, on the 30th, the Egyptian Air Force flew F16s over Cairo, as a show of strength by the military. On the 31st, the stock market and banks were closed, and most flights in and out of Egypt were canceled for security reasons. In Cairo, the main location for all the protests was the Tahrir Square, also known as Martyr Square, in downtown Cairo.

On the 1st of February, opposition leaders called for a "March of the Millions". The protesters were going to march from Tahrir Square to the Presidential palace, where police and military had installed barbed wire to keep rioters out of the facility. Later that evening, at around 11:00 pm Cairo time, Mubarak broadcast that he would not run for re-election in September 2011, when his term of office was up. However, he wanted to stay in office until then, to insure a peaceful transition of power to the next president. This was not good enough for the protesters, who wanted him out immediately.

Estimates of the actual number of marchers who assembled and proceeded towards the Palace ranged from one hundred thousand to two million, depending on which organization added up the numbers. In other cities around the country, similar marches took place, and the Muslim Brotherhood certainly used the occasion to enhance their membership.

On the 2nd of February, battles between pro-Mubarak and opposition protesters took place in Cairo and Alexandria. Gunfire was heard and Molotov cocktails were thrown, resulting in many injuries. There were reports that some of the pro-Mubarak forces were off duty police and military people; however this could not be confirmed. Regardless, the violence continued throughout the day and into the night. International leaders, mainly in Europe and North America, called for the violence to stop and for Mubarak to step aside. Mubarak did not heed the calls for his resignation.

On the next day, Thursday the 3rd, it was more of the same, with anti-government protesters battling pro-Mubarak supporters, using sticks, Molotov cocktails and even guns. Deaths and injuries continued to mount. Both sides camped out in Tahrir Square during the night, even as the military tried to clear it. The military even had to clear an overpass near the center of Cairo, where pro-government forces were raining concrete blocks down on the protesters below. Battles also continued unabated in Alexandria, Suez, Mansoura, Port Said and other major cities.

Friday the 4th of February was called the "Friday of Departure" by organizers of the protests, and they planned again to march on the palace. Estimates placed the number of protesters at two million and several groups of Christians and other faiths formed human chains around those, who were praying to protect them. There were rumors that the Obama administration talked with Egyptian officials about President Mubarak stepping down immediately and turning power over to a transitional government. In Alexandria, an estimated one million Egyptians protested and threatened to march on Cairo.

Through the nights of February 4th and 5th, protesters continued to camp out in Tahrir Square. As the day progressed in Cairo, more protesters came out to join those that had camped in the night. The army, stating it was neutral, tried to take down many of the barricades in the Square. Rumors spread throughout the protesters that Mubarak had resigned, but he had not done so.

On the 6th of February, while the protests continued, Vice President Suleiman met with the opposition, including Mohamed Morsi of the Muslim Brotherhood. The Vice President agreed to set up a committee for an early March meeting, to study reforms to the constitution. Meanwhile, protesters, estimated to number up to one million, voiced their grievances in Tahrir Square and at other Cairo major landmarks.

Monday, the 7th of February was marked by protests during the funeral of a reporter, from the newspaper Al Tawuun. Ahmad Mohamed Mahmoud was a reporter who was taking photos on the 4th of February, when he was shot in Tahrir Square. Demands were made for an investigation into his death. On this day, the banks finally reopened after having been closed for some time, which allowed Egyptians to get some money. Google's executive in the Middle East was released. He had been in custody for a couple of weeks, because Twitter and Facebook were instrumental in helping to develop the protests.

While all these protests continued in Egypt, the Obama administration in Washington delayed military and economic assistance, in order to pressure Mubarak "to be kind" to the protesters. This is what President Carter did to the Iranian Shah in 1978-1979, and Iran ended up in a worse situation. Human Rights are non-existent under the religious leaders now ruling Iran. Obama was trying to throw Mubarak under the same bus, even though it was Obama who initially stirred up the trouble with his Apology tour, two years earlier.

When the sun rose on the 8th of February 2011, one million Egyptians gathered in central Cairo, to again demand Mubarak's resignation. Journalists joined this protest and called for greater freedom of the press. During the day, Mubarak's newly named Interior Minister, Mahmoud Wagdy, released thirty-four political prisoners, most of who belonged to the Muslim Brotherhood. Later in the day, on state television, Vice President Suleiman made some announcements including that planning was in progress to transfer power peacefully, that a committee would immediately study reforms, and that the requirements for a free election would be drawn up. He also warned that a coup d'état was possible, unless the leaders of the opposition were prepared to negotiate.

As the 9th of February dawned, protesters who had camped out in Tahrir Square, moved to the Parliament building demanding that the Assembly be dissolved. Government offices were evacuated, as the rioters gathered outside. Strikes were called by the labor unions in many major cities, such as Alexandria, Suez, Cairo and Port Said. The Muslim Brotherhood again called for Mubarak to step aside. One of the problems that Western leaders, including Obama, did not recognize, was that the Brotherhood was the only effective political organization, other than Mubarak's NDP. Just as Jimmy Carter did not realize that the religious leaders in Iran were the only organized opposition to the Shah, so Obama was naïve into thinking democracy would flourish, if only Mubarak would go. Egyptian Foreign Minister Gheit rejected requests by the Obama administration to eliminate the emergency law, and he accused the U.S. government of interference in the internal affairs of Egypt.

An Egyptian tank in Tahrir Square

On the 10th of February, the protesters were out in the streets again, calling for Mubarak's resignation. Rumors floated through the crowds that Mubarak was about to resign and that the Vice President was going to take over. This never happened on the 10th, and the people became even more visibly upset, shouting "Resign, Resign, Resign". Mubarak did say that while he remained President, he would transfer power to the Vice President and that certain emergency laws would be lifted. This was not enough change for the protesters as they wanted Mubarak out; period.

In the morning of the 11th of February 2011, protesters started to march on the presidential palace, which was surrounded by police and the military. Helicopters left the palace grounds, carrying Mubarak and his family to a nearby air force base. From there, they flew in an aircraft to their retreat in Sharm el-Sheikh, at the tip of the Sinai Peninsula. At around 6:00 pm local time, Vice President Suleiman announced over the radio and television that the presidency had been vacated and that the military would be running the country. Just as Jimmy Carter did to the Shah thirty-two years earlier, Obama had thrown Mubarak under the proverbial bus. Eight hundred to a few thousand deaths are attributed to the crack down on the demonstrations. No one is sure of the exact number.

When Obama heard the news of Mubarak's resignation, he praised the Egyptian revolution, even though he did not understand the consequences of the power vacuum. He naively stated, "Nothing less than genuine democracy will carry the day." Top U.S. Obama administration officials welcomed Mubarak's resignation, even though they didn't know what would replace Mubarak's government. Egypt, like most other Arab countries, had never had a history of true democracy.

Just as in Iran, a government came into power that was worse than Mubarak's. In a 2012 election, Mohamed Morsi, the Muslim Brotherhood candidate, became President and almost immediately acted dictatorially. He granted himself unlimited powers and gave himself the authority to legislate, without any judicial oversight or review. In other words he acted like a dictator, which is what Ayatollah Khomeini did in Iran.

His presidency lasted one year and, on the 3rd of July 2013, the military kicked him out of office and took over the reins of government. On the 1st of September 2013, prosecutors arrested and charged Mohamed Morsi with inciting deadly violence and other charges. He has basically been held incommunicado at a remote Navy base and is still awaiting trial.

Mubarak and his two sons were arrested and charged with various crimes. All the charges and/or verdicts have been dropped or overturned. Some of the charges are still outstanding in 2015, but in all cases, the charges will probably be dropped.

Situation Analysis:

It is claimed the so-called Arab Spring, which started in Tunisia at the end of 2010, was initiated by the Obama Cairo University speech named "A New Beginning" in June 2009. Some politicians called it an Apology tour by Obama, since he made excuses for all the supposedly American arrogance that he perceived in the past. Obama mentioned, as examples, the invasions of Arab countries and the coup that ousted Iran Prime Minister Mosaddegh in 1953. Of course, most Americans, and people of the Western powers disagree with his assessment of past history.

President Obama and Secretary of State Hillary Clinton were basically trying to **APPEASE** the Arab population in all the Muslim countries, as he made his apology tour. The problem is that all he did was to stir up a hornet's nest, without any strategies for filling the vacuums, when the dictatorial leaders were ousted. This was a problem in Iraq, when Saddam Hussein was ousted, and Bush had not sent enough troops to the country, so that order could be maintained.

This type of situation was avoided at the end of World War Two in Germany and Japan. General Douglas McArthur ran Japan for five years, until the democracy flourished and he could leave. In Germany, the US, France and Britain ran the government with the help of anti-Nazi Germans, like Konrad Adenauer and Ludwig Erhard.

President Jimmy Carter helped oust the Shah of Iran, because he didn't like the Shah's human rights record. What Carter ended up with was an autocratic one party religious country that has no respect for women or human rights. On top of that, they have their secret police and execute many more people per year, than the Shah ever did.

Barack Obama and Hillary Clinton conducted the same **BLUNDER** with Egypt. Mubarak was probably not the nicest of leaders, but he did keep stability in the region. By helping oust Mubarak, Obama and Clinton received in return the Muslim Brotherhood President Morsi, who was worse than Mubarak. They did not realize or didn't care that the Muslim Brotherhood was the only organized political party which could win in an election. Morsi ignored the assembly and the courts, and took absolute power for himself.

This upheaval in Egypt has created a ripple or domino effect that is sweeping the Arab world. By **BLUNDERING** and **APPEASING**, Obama is trying to please the left leaning socialist elite of the world, like George Soros. As you will read in the next few chapters, Libya, Syria, Iraq, Yemen, Afghanistan could all go through the throes of chaos and end up with unstable governments. On top of this, Obama and current Secretary of State John Kerry now have on their hands the ISIS, ISIL or whatever you want to call those Islamic terrorists.

Whenever, one ousts or assists in the ouster of a government or leader, you had better be prepared to fill the vacuum with a better alternative.

The Kennedy administration approved the coup that ousted President Ngo Dinh Diem, but he didn't have a good alternative, except for some South Vietnamese generals who squabbled amongst themselves. The Truman administration did not help Chiang Kai-shek in his battle with the Communists, and it ended up with a regime that was a lot worse than the somewhat corrupt Nationalist government.

Overall, the ouster of a friendly government, like Egypt's Mubarak, is generally a disaster waiting to happen. Usually, there is a power vacuum that is filled by someone or some organization. First, Obama got Morsi who wanted to be a dictator himself and was not friendly to Israel. Then, when Morsi was ousted by the military, Obama and Kerry got a military government in power that they did not like.

What do they do? They cut off military and economic aid, and pushed the Egyptian government into the arms of Russia and Putin. Russia is more than happy to provide arms to Egypt, since it gives Putin influence in the Middle East, as he has in Syria.

APPEASEMENT, as noted in chapter three, does not work and only puts off the day of reckoning.

15

Libyan Crisis & Civil War
2011

On the 1st of September 1969, a group of army officers, led by Colonel Muammar Gaddafi, conducted a coup d'état and ousted the ruling Libyan monarch, King Idris. Colonel Gaddafi ran the country for the next forty-two years, using the oil money (oil was discovered in 1959) to finance his own bank account and to build up the Libyan armed forces. It was important to him to keep the armed forces well funded, since they helped keep him in power.

During the years 1969 to 2010, Gaddafi ran Libya as a dictator, and he was known for supporting terrorism, mainly in Europe and the Middle East. In 1970, Libya kicked the U.S. and Britain out of their respective air bases in Tripoli (Wheelus AFB) and Tobruk. Gaddafi also nationalized the oil industry and forced many American companies to leave the country. The oil industry provided most of the revenue for Libya from 1959 onwards. The oil fields were further developed from 1965-1986, with the help of the U.S. Occidental Petroleum Company.

Sixteen years later, on the 24th of March 1986, there was a naval clash in the Gulf of Sedra. The Libyans claimed that the Gulf was Libyan territory and they had drawn an imaginary "line of death" in the water. The U.S. stated that the waters were open to all shipping, under international maritime laws, and America had the right to operate in the area. The Libyans sent some ships out to challenge the U.S. carrier group, and four of the Libyan craft were ultimately destroyed, after threatening the U.S. vessels.

Then, twelve days later, on the 5th of April 1986, a bomb exploded in La Belle Discotheque, located in Berlin, that was frequented by American servicemen stationed in Germany. Two U.S. servicemen were killed and around 79 were injured in the bomb blast. It was presumed that the bombing was in retaliation for the sinking of the four ships. Regardless, President Reagan immediately placed sanctions on Libya.

Colonel Gaddafi
with
President Nasser
of Egypt
in 1969

Timeline of Events in Modern Day Libya

DATES	EVENTS
24 December 1951	United Kingdom of Libya was given its freedom and it became their Independence Day
24 December 1951	Idris as-Senussi became King Idris 1 of Libya
1 September 1969	Colonel Muammar Gaddafi deposed King Idris in a coup, while the king was in Turkey
5 April 1986	"La Belle" discotheque was bombed in Berlin and investigation pointed finger at Libya
25 April 1986	President Reagan approved strike by US aircraft on Libya in response to disco bomb
21 December 1988	Pan Am flight 103 (Boeing 747) was blown up in the skies over Lockerbie, Scotland
19 December 2003	Libya agreed to destroy all chemical stocks after seeing what happened in Iraq
19 December 2003	Libya agreed to the UN nuclear controls and turned over nuclear material
15 February 2011	Benghazi violence erupted after human rights advocate was arrested by Libyan Government
17 March 2011	United Nations authorized no-fly zone over Libya and NATO assumed command
19 March 2011	Coalition started military intervention, including no-fly zone, led by France and UK
24 March 2011	NATO agreed to take over control of the no-fly zone on 31 March
31 March 2011	NATO officially took over control of the no-fly zone
15 July 2011	National Transitional Council recognized by ICG as the Government of Libya
24 August 2011	Gaddafi compound in Tripoli was overrun by the rebels and Gaddafi fled
20 October 2011	Colonel Muammar Gaddafi was cornered, captured and killed by Libyans
31 October 2011	NATO ended military operations, including no-fly zone, in Libya
12 September 2012	Ambassador Stevens was killed as the U.S. Embassy in Benghazi was ransacked

Nine days after the bombing in Berlin, on the 14th of April, the U.S. bombed strategic targets in Libya, killing 101 people, including the adopted daughter of the Libyan president. Muammar Gaddafi immediately ousted the American Occidental Oil Company from Libya, and it was not able to return until twenty-five years later. Gaddafi plotted revenge for the death of his daughter and the attack.

Two and one half years later, on the 21st of December 1988, Pan American 103 flying from Frankfurt to Detroit, via JFK, blew up over Scotland at an altitude of 31,000 feet, with the loss of all 243 passengers and the 16 crew on board. Eleven Scots, on the ground, were also killed by the debris raining down on them. A long, drawn-out investigation determined some agents of the Libyan secret service were responsible for checking a bag, containing the bomb, in Malta, and later it was transferred onto the Pan Am flight in Frankfurt.

In 1992, the United Nations imposed sanctions on Libya, in an effort to force Gaddafi to hand over the responsible men, for trial. Seven years later, in 1999, the two suspects were handed over to authorities in the Netherlands. They were then transferred to Scotland for trial, where they were found guilty and sentenced to prison.

In September 2003, the United Nations lifted the sanctions on Libya, after the U.S. had invaded Iraq and ousted Saddam Hussein. In December 2003, Libya abandoned its nuclear and chemical programs, after they saw how quickly the Americans, under President George W. Bush, destroyed the Iraqi army.

From 2004 to the beginning of 2011, life went on as normal in Libya, with the dictator Gaddafi still running the country and collecting the oil revenue. At the end of 2010, the so-called "Arab Spring" commenced in Tunisia and started to spread throughout North Africa.

On the afternoon of the 15th of February 2011, a Libyan lawyer, by the name of Fathi Tarbal, was arrested by Libyan security forces for his activities, in trying to protect the Human Rights of imprisoned activists from Benghazi. The next day, protests broke out in Benghazi, which was the second largest city in Libya. The protesters called for the release of Fathi Tarbal. Thus, the Libyan civil war began and it continued for nine months, during which time it tore the country apart and created a political, power vacuum.

During the next three days, 17th, 18th and 19th of February, the demonstrations grew and spread to other cities, including the capital Tripoli. Some shooting by security forces took place, which resulted in several deaths. Several Libyan government officials, ambassadors and representatives resigned, in protest with the Government's position. Even Gaddafi's son, Saif, got into the act and stated his father would fight to the last bullet.

On the 21st of February, two Libyan air force Dassault jet fighters flew across the Mediterranean Sea to the island of Malta, where the pilots asked for political asylum. On the same day, the United Nations Secretary General met with Gaddafi and insisted the violence cease. By evening, the rebels in Benghazi claimed that they had control of the eastern part of Libya.

Libyan Mirage F1 in Malta

Photo by Ron Schleiffert

The violence persisted and, on the 25th of February, the American Embassy in the country was closed and the American government froze the assets of Gaddafi that he had deposited in American banks. By the 28th of the month, Europe also froze Gaddafi's assets, imposed sanctions on Libya and enacted an arms embargo.

On the 7th of March, NATO started an air surveillance mission of Libyan airspace and, on the 17th of March, the United Nations Security Council imposed a no-fly zone over the country. In the meantime, violence continued between the government security forces and the rebels. On the 19th of March, French planes started to enforce the no-fly zone, and the U.S. launched over 100 tomahawk missiles, from ships offshore in the Mediterranean, at key Libyan military and communication targets.

On the 24th of March 2011, NATO agreed to take command of the no-fly zone, in place over Libya. The U.S. did not play any leadership role in the battle by the rebels or NATO, in the fight against Gaddafi. Five days later, the Italian Foreign Minister Frattini stated that they were seeking a sanctuary for Gaddafi, in order to encourage him to leave Libya. However, Gaddafi had seen what happened to Hosni Mubarak of Egypt, Saddam Hussein of Iraq and the Shah of Iran, he decided to stay put and fight to the end.

On the 2nd of April, NATO airstrikes hit a rebel column by mistake (friendly fire) and killed at least twelve rebel partisans. During April, the rebels shipped their first load of Libyan oil in a tanker and received the revenue. At the end of the month, on the 30th of April, NATO planes bombed a house in Tripoli, killing Gaddafi's youngest son, Saif al-Arab, and three of Saif's children. On the same day, Gaddafi declared he was ready to negotiate with the rebels, but he would not resign the office of President.

During the month of May, the violence continued with an attack by pro-Gaddafi forces on the British and Italian Tripoli Embassies, in retaliation for the death of Gaddafi's son. NATO fighters again bombed a Gaddafi compound, this time in Bab al-Aziziyah, killing a few people, but not harming the Libyan president himself. The rebels kept advancing towards Tripoli and captured the airport at Misrata, located about one hundred miles east of Tripoli.

On the 1st of June 2011, NATO extended its no-fly zone for another ninety days and, on the 18th, the rebel oil chief, Ali Tarhouni, claimed that the opposition had run out of money, despite pledges by the Western powers. The United States House of Representatives threatened to withhold funds for the U.S. forces activity, unless the Obama administration came to Congress to obtain approval for its military operation. The U.S. was still leading from behind and left it up to the European nations, to conduct the operation against Gaddafi. The Obama administration argued that since the U.S. was only in a supporting role, approval by Congress was not required. Republican's claimed that President Obama was exceeding his authority, by waging war against another country.

In July 2011, the Obama administration officially recognized the National Transitional Council as the legitimate government of Libya, even though some of its members belonged to the Muslim Brotherhood or Ansar al-Sharia. On the 27th of July, Great Britain also recognized the National Transitional Council (NTC), as the official governing body of Libya. One day later, General Abdul Fattah Younis, the NTC top military commander, was assassinated in an ambush. The rumor was that he was killed by the more extreme rebels, because he was not one of them and he might be a threat to them in the future. In addition, there was another rumor that it was a revenge killing, since General Younis had been a general in Gaddafi's army, before defecting to the rebels.

The civil war continued into August and September 2011, with the rebels advancing on the capital Tripoli. By the 23rd of August, the NTC claimed they controlled over eighty percent of the capital city. On the 29th of August, it was announced by the rebels that Gaddafi's son, Khamis, had been killed in a gun battle, and Algerian authorities reported that Gaddafi's wife, along with some children and grandchildren, had taken refuge in their country.

In September 2011, fighting between Gaddafi loyalists and the rebel army of the NTC continued, in and around Sirte. The NTC was recognized by most countries during the month, and it sent its first representative to the United Nations. On the 24th of the month, the NTC Prime Minister Mahmoud Jibril addressed the United Nations General Assembly for the first time.

Sporadic fighting continued through the beginning of October, and the rebels hunted Gaddafi, and his sons, for the first part of October. Finally, on the 20th of October 2011, President Muammar Gaddafi was killed by the rebels, as he tried to escape in a convoy from his home town of Sirte. He was actually found in a drainage ditch still alive, but when he arrived at a hospital, he was dead. It is still uncertain whether he was assassinated, or died from injuries he received when the convoy was attacked. Regardless, Muammar Gaddafi, the dictator of Libya, was dead.

On the 27th of October, the United Nations Security Council voted to cease all military activity at the end of the month. Four days later, the NATO Secretary General announced that, as of the 31st of October, all NATO military operations would cease, and the forces would return to their respective countries. Thus, the NATO operation against Gaddafi ended, but it left a huge vacuum in the country, since most of the power was in the hands of the extreme groups, who were well armed. This situation would lead to a major attack on the U.S. embassy almost a year later (see chapter seventeen).

Situation Analysis:

Before the leader of a country is eliminated or forced to leave, along with the power structure that holds the country together, you had better figure out how you will control events and put an administration in place. The U.S. made a mess of things in Iran, Iraq and Egypt, and now the Libyan power structure for the past forty years was going to be removed. The NATO mission had no clear leader, and started out in chaos, with an attack by French Rafale fighter jets on a Gaddafi tank column approaching Benghazi.

American U-2s flew out of the British RAF Akrotiri air base on Cyprus, to help enforce the no-fly zone over Libya. In addition, the top floor of the U.S. Embassy in Nicosia was a data collecting and processing base for SIGINT information, from Libya and other Middle East countries. This signal monitoring also included communications picked up from the terrorist organizations such as al-Qaeda, Hezbollah, Hamas and Ansar al-Sharia. The SIGINT monitoring base at Ayios Nikolaos run by the British and Americans in Cyprus, also participated in this data collection. Ayios Nikolaos is located in the British SBA (Sovereign Base Area) at Dhekelia, which Britain negotiated with Cyprus in the London-Zurich Agreement of 1959.

The U.S., under President Obama, followed a policy of "lead from behind". In any previous military engagements before 2008, the U.S. organized and led coalitions. In the case of Libya, the U.S. did not lead, and there was no strategy for controlling Libya, once the Gaddafi government was overthrown. This was a major **BLUNDER** on the part of NATO and the U.S. It turns out that Secretary of State, Hillary Clinton, wanted to rush into a war and overthrow the Gaddafi regime, regardless of the consequences (See Chapter 17). The Joint Chief of Staff at the Pentagon tried to stop her by negotiating with Gaddafi and his son Seif. They foresaw a major vacuum being created and that it would be filled by Islamic terrorists.

Libya had been taken off the list of state sponsors of terrorism, under the Bush administration. Gaddafi had compensated Pan AM 103 passenger relatives and, as pointed out earlier, Libya had given up its chemical and nuclear programs. President Obama and Hillary Clinton were not interested in negotiating any kind of settlement, but wanted a regime change. They wanted to throw Gaddafi under the bus, as they had Mubarak in Egypt, a few days before.

President Obama authorized the CIA to give arms to Al Qaeda, in order to help in the overthrow of the Gaddafi regime. This was similar to what was done in Afghanistan in the 1980's against the USSR. The problem is getting the arms back once the regime, you are trying to overthrow, is eliminated. The Obama administration also failed to stop a massive arms shipment by the UAE, from reaching the Islamic militants.

As was predictable, since the overthrow of the Gaddafi government, there has been infighting between the various parties that are now claiming the right to set up a government. Various militias are fighting amongst themselves, and Islamic terrorists, including ISIS, are trying to obtain a major foothold in the country. Since Libya has an oil industry of some considerable size, control of the oil fields gives the holders, the funds with which to finance their militia.

In less than one year after the death of Gaddafi, there was an attack on the United States Embassy located in Benghazi during which four Americans, including the ambassador, were killed. As mentioned earlier, this power vacuum created by the elimination of the Gaddafi power structure, no matter how onerous it was, allowed undesirable groups to take a hold in the various Libyan cities.

The U.S. had no idea who was going to control Libya after Gaddafi, and the Obama administration did not seem to care. It was "missing in action", and just followed the NATO lead. The problem was who was leading the NATO mission?

The major issue with Libya is that the country was basically unified by the Italians in the 1930s. Before that time, the area consisted of tribes, run by tribal leaders. There is the potential, with all the different militias fighting for power, the country could break apart. Other Arab countries are not helping, as they are supporting different militias or Islamists. Qatar, the UAE, Iran and Saudi Arabia are all trying to influence the outcome, with Shiite Iran and Sunni Saudi Arabia not being on the best of terms.

In some ways, Libya is becoming a microcosm of what ails the Middle East. The U.S. and Europe has no desire to get back into the fray, as they would become the targets of all the militias. Tripoli, the capital, is currently held by the Libyan Dawn, which some analysts equate to ISIS/ISIL. It is not a pretty picture, and it is all because the Obama administration, and NATO, did not have a strategy in place to control the area, after destroying Gaddafi.

On the 27th of January 2015, almost four years to the day since the start of the Libyan revolt, a group of Islamic terrorists claiming to be part of ISIS attacked the Corinthia luxury hotel in Tripoli. At least ten foreigners, including one American were killed in this attack, a symptom of what happens when a vacuum is created by the removal of a government, without firm plans to replace it.

16

Iraq Civil War
2011 to 2014

Around dawn, on the 18th of December 2011, the United States pulled its last troops out of Iraq, since the Obama administration had not negotiated a treaty, whereby a residual force could remain, to help maintain security and order. The convoy of approximately five hundred U.S. soldiers crossed over the border, from Iraq into Kuwait. Just four days later, on the 22nd of December 2011, ISI (Islamic State of Iraq), under the leadership of Abu Bakr al-Baghadi, conducted some car bombings and IED attacks in Baghdad, killing at least seventy Iraqis and wounding over one hundred and fifty. In addition, there were attacks in Mosul and Kirkuk that also killed a few people.

This was a foretelling of what was to come in a country, divided mainly by three different groups; the Sunnis, the Shia and the Kurds. In the years after World War One, Iraq was made a country, out of parts of the Ottoman Empire. The three sects have no love for each other and, when Obama pulled the U.S. troops out, old animosities came to the surface.

During the next three years, the Iraq insurgency intensified and became a civil war; pitting, Kurds, Shiite Muslims and Sunni Muslims, including ISIS/ISIL, against one another. Prime Minister Nouri al-Maliki, a Shia, was ineffective as a leader and did not foster cooperation between the religious sects. In fact, he got closer to Iran that was also a Shiite based country. This caused many problems with the Sunni Muslims, who staged protests across Iraq.

During 2012, the first year after the U.S. withdrew its troops from Iraq, the violence increased dramatically. In January 2012 alone, large Shiite areas were targeted with bombings and gun attacks; probably by Sunnis or al-Qaeda. It is estimated more than 200 people, who were mainly Shia, were killed in the month of January. An arrest warrant for the Iraqi Vice President Tariq al-Hashemi, a Sunni Muslim, was issued by the Maliki Shiite government. He was accused of using death squads for murder and corruption, carried out between 2006 and 2011.

An Arab League summit meeting was held in Baghdad, during the 27th to 29th of March 2012, and an upsurge of suicide attacks and bombings took place in the capital, prior to the meeting. These assaults caused the deaths of dozens of Iraqis, and the wounding of many more.

On the 2nd of April, Iraqi Kurdistan stopped oil exports, after an argument with the Maliki central government, over payment disputes and the contracts involving overseas companies. Baghdad claimed only it had the right to export oil, while the Kurds insisted that they could export oil from their land.

Timeline of Events Post Iraq War

DATES	EVENTS
19 March 2003	President George W Bush commenced a military campaign to oust Saddam Hussein
15 June 2007	The US surge commenced and ultimately pacified most of Iraq
27 February 2009	Obama administration announced that the US combat mission ends 31 August 2010
17 October 2011	Leon Panetta still pushed for a troop extension to insure security in Iraq
18 December 2011	Last US troops withdrawn from Iraq by Obama administration
23 July 2012	107 Iraqis killed by bombs in Baghdad and the North in one day
23 April 2013	Iraqi troops, mostly Shia, stormed a Sunni anti-government protest camp
21 July 2013	500 prisoners, mostly al-Qaeda escaped from prisons in a planned attack by al-Qaeda
4 January 2014	ISIS/ISIL captured the Iraqi town of Fallujah after driving Iraqi forces into flight
10 June 2014	ISIS/ISIL captured Mosul after the Iraqi forces fled the city
15 June 2014	President Obama ordered 180 US troops dispatched to Iraq
30 June 2014	US increased non-combat troop strength in Iraq from the 180 to 480
5 August 2014	US started to supply arms to the Kurds in Northern Iraq
8 August 2014	US commenced airstrikes against ISIS/ISIL in Iraq
14 August 2014	Maliki resigned as Iraqi Prime Minister and was replaced by Haidar al-Abadi
18 August 2014	ISIS/ISIL driven from the Mosul dam that they had captured earlier in year
20 August 2014	James Foley, a US photojournalist, was executed by ISIS in the Iraqi desert
10 September 2014	US sent 500 more non-combat troops to Iraq to provide aid to Iraqi army
30 September 2014	US troop strength increased to approximately1600
7 November 2014	US troops strength increased again and 1500 more non-combat troops announced

The violence continued unabated throughout the year 2012. In June of that year alone, more than 165 Iraqis were slaughtered. On the 23rd of July, there were a series of attacks that targeted the security forces and Shiites in up to eighteen cities and towns in all, including Baghdad, Taji, Sadr City and Mosul.

These July attacks were a major escalation of the violence by the minority Sunnis and other disenchanted Iraqis, against the Shiite governing majority. The number of attacks was estimated to be between thirty and forty, on this one day alone.

Then, on Sunday the 9th of September, the Iraqi Vice President, Tariq al-Hashami, was convicted in absentia and sentenced to be hung, for the murder of Iraqi Shia. He had been accused of using death squads, and he fled to Turkey before he could be arrested. After the verdict was handed down, Sunnis attacked the Shia, with the result that thirty were killed and ninety were wounded. The violence continued into October and November, 2012.

On the 10th of November 2012, Iraq cancelled a contract with the Russian Federation for weapons, consisting of helicopters and missiles. It had only been signed the month before, on the 9th of October, and would have made Russia the second largest arms supplier to Iraq, behind the United States. It was cancelled by the government, on concerns about corruption within the agency handling the contract. It was also rumored that the contract was cancelled, due to opposition from the U.S. government.

On the 18th of December 2012, the President of Iraq, Kurdish politician Jalai Talabani, suffered a stroke and two days later had recovered sufficiently to allow his transportation to Germany for further treatment. The office was basically ceremonial, so his absence from Iraq was not of major concern. As it turned out, he remained in Germany for one and one half years and did not return to Iraq, until the 19th of July 2014. He resigned the presidency due to his health, just five days later, on the 24th of July. He was replaced by another Kurdish politician Faud Masum.

The year 2013 saw intensified violence across the entire country. Suicide bombings and attacks by militants occurred almost daily, somewhere in Iraq. The Sunnis claimed that the Shiite government led by Maliki, a Shea, was discriminating against the Sunni minority. On the 8th of March, police killed a Sunni demonstrator in Mosul, and on the 10th of March, an anti-government demonstrator was shot and killed in Kirkuk.

On the 23rd of April 2013, Iraqi troops stormed a Sunni protest camp in the town of Hawija, located close to Kirkuk, and killed at least fifty Sunnis. These killings caused outrage across the Sunni areas of Iraq, creating riots and protests in other towns and cities. The protests, riots and killings continued into May and June, so that by July, the level of violence had reached a climax, and journalists were calling it a civil war.

On the 21st of July, there was a major attack on the Baghdad Central Prison, by the ISIL organization. They used car bombs, suicide bombers, rockets and mortars to gain entry. Approximately five hundred prisoners escaped, most of who were senior al-Qaeda members, under life or death sentences. At the same time, a simultaneous attack on a jail in Taji, released another ten to twenty prisoners. It seemed that most of the escapees joined ISIL, whose strength was increasing by the day.

On the 1st of September, there was a raid by supposedly Iraqi forces on Camp Ashraf that housed Iranian dissidents, many of who belonged to the PMOI/MEK organizations. The People's Mojahedin Organization of Iran, commonly known as Mujahedeen-e-Khalq, is a controversial resistance group to the current State of Iran. This may have been a false flag operation conducted mainly by Iranian troops, dressed as Iraqis. Regardless, fifty two dissidents were killed, and it is rumored some living rebels were taken to Iran to be questioned, and then executed. There were international protests about the attack, but nothing came of them.

At the end of October, the Iraq government issued a report stating that October was the worst month for violence, since 2008. They claimed over 900 Iraqis were killed in the month, and many more wounded from bombings and shootings. On the 25th of December 2013, Christmas Day, there were at least three separate bombings in Baghdad that targeted Christian Churches. In all, over thirty eight people were killed and over seventy were wounded in the bombings, and no group claimed responsibility.

The year 2014 saw a major change in Iraq, with the spillover of violence from the Syrian civil war that had been waged since 2011. ISIS (Islamic State of Iraq and Syria), also known as ISIL, started to take over segments of Iraq. They invaded Iraq military bases and towns, capturing heavy weapons and stealing money from the banks. This money helped ISIS to bankroll their operation, along with illegal sales of oil from their territory.

The first five months of 2014 saw skirmishes between the Iraq government forces and ISIS. In early January, ISIS took Fallujah and parts of Ramadi, and they battled Iraqi forces to hold on to them. All this fighting came to a head on the 5th of June 2014, when ISIS attacked and captured Samarra. This was followed by ISIS capturing Mosul, on the 10th of June, and taking over Tikrit, Saddam Hussein's hometown, on the next day. In many cases, when ISIS advanced on Iraqi army positions, the Iraqi army personnel fled, leaving their weapons behind.

On the 15th of June, the Obama administration announced that they were sending 180 non-combat troops back into Iraq, to train and support Iraqi security forces. On the 30th of June, President Obama disclosed that he was sending another additional 300 non-combat troops to assist Iraq in its fight to take back areas, captured by ISIS.

Events in Iraq came to a head in August 2014, when ISIS took control of the Mosul Dam on the 7th, after a fierce battle with the Iraqi defenders. The Obama administration agreed to start air combat missions, to help the Iraqi army in its fight against ISIS. On the 8th of August 2014, the U.S. and British aircraft went into action, for the first time, against ISIS, bombing targets of opportunity. The air missions targeted the ISIS defenders at the Mosul

Dam, and by the 18th, the Iraqi and Kurdish forces had managed to retake the Dam.

On the 19th of August 2014, the first American, John Foley, was beheaded by ISIS, who claimed it was in response to the air attacks by American aircraft. The U.S. renewed its attacks on ISIS and planned to launch attacks against the Islamic terrorists in Syria. On the 22nd of September, the U.S., with other nations, started to bomb ISIS targets in Syria. However, the Obama administration never developed a strategy for defeating ISIS.

During 2014, Prime Minister Maliki came under increasing pressure to step down, due to the lack of support by Iraqis and their faith in his ability to counter the ISIS threat. On the 8th of September, after considerable pressure was applied by the Obama administration and other countries, Maliki stepped down as Prime Minister. Haidar al-Abadi was elected in his place, by the Iraqi parliament.

On the 10th of September 2014, Obama announced an additional 500 troops would head for Iraq, and on the 30th he stated that another 600 troops would be sent, bringing the total to around 1580. Then on the 7th of November, President Obama announced that an additional 1500 troops would also be sent to Iraq. He had stated previously in a speech that he would never send ground troops to Iraq. The 3,000 troops would be non-combat and would be used for security and training purposes only. This sounded like *mission creep* to many military observers.

While all of this was going on, ISIS renamed itself and said it was now called Islamic State (IS), and

169

declared a caliphate. A caliphate is a form of Islamic government led by a caliph. The caliph is a person considered a political and religious successor to the Prophet Muhammed. Whatever they called themselves did not alter the fact that IS controlled major parts of Syria and Iraq. They appeared to have the funds to finance their operation and the heavy weapons, with which to carry on the fight.

On the 27th of January 2015, a FlyDubai aircraft, flight 215, was struck by small-arms fire as it landed in Baghdad. Whether this was an accident or intentional waits to be seen.

Situation Analysis:

After the U.S. eliminated Saddam Hussein and the Sunni run government, a power vacuum was created that the Shia were not prepared to fill. On top of that, the Sunni felt that they would be discriminated against, and they prepared to conduct an insurgency against the Americans and the Shia. The Obama administration made the situation worse by not negotiating a treaty to keep a residual force in place. When the U.S. finally did pull all of its troops out at the end of 2011, they left a country that was unprepared to govern itself and provide security to its people. On top of that, America left a country that contained three major religious sects, none of which trusted each other.

For unclear reasons and against military advice, Obama had announced well in advance, the U.S. troops withdrawal date. This made it simple for the terrorists to plan their attacks. President Obama, and his advisor Valerie Jarrett, probably made this announcement, so that they could satisfy their supporters, in the liberal base of their party. Just four days after the last troops departed, a major attack by some Islamic extremists took place.

Obama received considerably advice from the military leaders involved with the Iraq situation, but ignored all of it, because he was naïve, incompetent and thought he knew better. Pulling all United Sates troops, out at the end of 2011, was a major **BLUNDER** by President Obama. Then, when ISIS started to rear its ugly head in 2013 and 2014, the President realized the error of his ways, but he could not admit it. Finally, after ISIS captured Mosul and threatened Baghdad, President Obama announced the reintroduction of non-combat troops into Iraq, and then he continued sending more troops into action, over the next four months. This amounted to *Mission Creep* which was tried in Vietnam and did not work.

What would happen if ISIS captured just one of the American non-combat soldiers and threatened to cut off his head? No declaration has been made by the White House on this subject.

In August 2014, the first American civilian did lose his head just days after the U.S. commenced air missions against ISIS in Iraq. However, the White House would still not use the words "Islamic Terrorists" to describe ISIS. This amounted to **APPEASEMENT**. If you cannot describe who your enemies are, how can you hope to defeat them?

In World War Two, we described who the enemy was – Nazi Germany – and we defeated them. Every soldier in the U.S. army knew who the enemy was, and why they should be defeated.

The current U.S. military does not know who the enemy is and what the strategy is to defeat them. How can our soldiers be expected to win in this situation? We hand over five Islamic Terrorists for one U.S. deserter, and we expect to win. The White House has claimed that the United States would not negotiate with Taliban terrorists, but we did to get a deserter back.

The situation in Iraq is going to be with us for a long time, since Iran is going to keep stirring the pot. Iran's goal is to take over the entire Middle East with its oil. Unless America, and the rest of the "West", comes up with a strategy to win, the next twenty to twenty-five years are going to be very troubling, to say the least.

Already, Yemen is collapsing and al-Qaeda will develop havens there, for attacks on the West. In fact they already have a history of doing just that.

The U.S. pulled out of Iraq too early, and it should not have been announced ahead of time. The U.S. is now doing the same thing in Afghanistan. We announced the withdrawal of troops by a certain date so, if you are the Taliban leader, you just wait for the opportune time to attack; probably spring 2015.

Iraq is a symptom of what ails the Middle East. Terrorists flourish everywhere and most religious sects hate each other enough, to go on a vendetta. The Obama administration is loathe to admit who the enemy is.

17

Benghazi, Libya
2012

J. Christopher Stevens, the United States Ambassador to Libya, was pronounced dead at 2:00 am local time on the 12th of September 2012, at a Benghazi hospital. He had been taken to the hospital in a state of cardiac arrest, due to smoke inhalation suffered, when the U.S. Embassy in Benghazi came under attack from Islamic terrorists and militias. This attack, under the cover of darkness, started at approximately 9:40 pm on the 11th of September and lasted for about two hours.

A second attack took place just after midnight on the CIA annex, 1.2 miles away from the Embassy, and ended before dawn. The attackers in both raids used mortars, hand grenades, AK-47s and trucks with machine guns mounted on them. The attackers also brought cans of flammable liquids with them, so they could set fire to the buildings.

In all, four Americans died, including Ambassador Stevens, and up to seven men were wounded; in addition seven Libyan guards were thought to have suffered wounds during the attacks. The other dead

Americans were Sean Smith (Foreign Service Information Management Officer), Tyrone Woods and Glen Doherty, both CIA contractors.

Ever since the downfall and death of Muammar Gaddafi in October 2011, Libya had been in a state of crisis. Various militant and terrorist organizations roamed the country, and Libya did not have an effective central government. NATO, including the Obama administration, had no effective plan to fill the vacuum, caused by the removal of Gaddafi. Chapter fifteen of this book covered the downfall of Gaddafi. Throughout the first part of 2012, there were plenty of signs of the breakdown in law and order in the country.

On the 10th of April 2012, an improvised explosive device (IED) was thrown at a convoy, carrying the United Nations Special Envoy to Libya through Benghazi. No Islamic terrorist group claimed responsibility for the attack, and no one was arrested. On the 19th of April, Secretary of State Hillary Clinton put her signature to a plan proposal that called for the decrease in security at U.S. missions in Libya, including the one in Benghazi. Consulates are often called Special Missions, in terminology used by the Department of State.

In the early morning hours of the 22nd of May, two rocket propelled grenades (RPG) were fired at the ICRC (International Committee of the Red Cross) building in Benghazi. Luckily, they did not cause any injuries, because of the early hours and no one was at work. The ICRC building was damaged considerably, but it was still usable.

Timeline Leading up to Benghazi Attack and Aftermath

DATES	EVENTS
4 June 2009	US President Obama gave apology speech "A New Beginning" at Cairo University
25 January 2011	Mass protests started against Mubarak in Cairo and continued for 18 days
11 February 2011	President Mubarak suddenly resigned even though he stated he would stay until Sept.
15 February 2011	Benghazi violence erupted as human rights advocate was arrested by Libyan Govt.
20 October 2011	Colonel Muammar Gaddafi was cornered, captured and killed by Libyans
31 October 2011	NATO ended military operations, including no-fly zone, in Libya
10 June 2012	British Ambassador in Benghazi narrowly escaped assassination attempt
30 June 2012	Muhammad Morsi of the Moslem Brotherhood became President of Egypt
1 July 2012	Anti-Islamic video "Innocence of Muslims" first posted on You Tube
6 August 2012	I.C.R.C suspended operations in Benghazi due to deteriorating security conditions
15 August 2012	Cable sent to Hillary Clinton stated Benghazi embassy could not be defended from attack
11 September 2012	Rioting outside the American Embassy in Cairo demanding release of blind Sheikh
11 September 2012	At 2140 hours, armed men attacked the US embassy in Benghazi
11 September 2012	POTUS informed by Leon Panetta 1700 EST terrorists have attacked Benghazi embassy
11 September 2012	Ambassador Stevens and FORD killed in first raid on the U.S. Embassy in Benghazi
12 September 2012	Relief unit told to "stand down, you need to wait" by "Bob" CIA station chief
12 September 2012	At 0400 hours, a second attack on the CIA annex one mile away took place
12 September 2012	Two other Americans killed in this second attack on the Benghazi CIA compound
16 September 2012	Susan Rice went on five TV networks and blamed the attack on the anti-Islamic video
6 November 2012	Obama won reelection over Mitt Romney with major claim that Al-Qaeda defeated
23 January 2013	Hillary Clinton testified to Congress said - What difference, at this point, does it make?

On the 10th of June, the British Ambassador Dominic Asquith was travelling to the British Benghazi Consulate Office, when his convoy was hit by a rocket propelled grenade (RPG), approximately 300 yards from the building. Two British bodyguards were injured in the attack, and as a result of the attack and the deteriorating situation, the British Foreign Office withdrew all consular staff, by the end of June. Just eight days later, on the 18th of June 2012, the Tunisian consulate in Benghazi was attacked by members of the Ansar Al Sharia terrorist group, because they objected to Tunisian artists' representation of Islam.

The International Committee of the Red Cross decided that the situation was getting so bad that they suspended operations in Benghazi, on the 6th of August 2012. Due to the increasing activity by the Islamic terrorist organizations, Eric Nordstrom, U.S. Security Officer for the State Department, repeatedly asked for added security and was turned down. It appeared that the State Department official Charlene Lamb wanted to keep a low security profile. Secretary of State Hillary Clinton later accepted responsibility for the security lapses.

On the actual day of the attack, the 11th of September 2012, two Benghazi consulate guards observed a man dressed in a Libyan police uniform (maybe a false flag operation) taking pictures of the consulate facility, from a nearby building. They went and talked with him, before letting him go off in his police car. They made a complaint about this man to the local police station. This day of infamy and tragedy (9/11) will be remembered, not only for the

New York twin tower destruction, but also for the death of four brave American men in Benghazi.

The following is a timeline (times listed are local Benghazi time) of the attack on the Special Mission (Benghazi consulate) and the CIA Annex.

11 September 2012

9:40 pm: The attack started on the Special Mission. U.S. Ambassador Christopher Stevens called the number two U.S. man in Libya and told him that they were under attack.

10:05 pm: The State Department Operations Center issued an alert to all agencies stating that the U.S. diplomatic mission in Benghazi was under attack.

10:25 pm: Six member CIA team, under Tyrone Woods, left the Annex and arrived at the Special Mission about 1.2 miles away. They found the body of Sean Smith but could not find Stevens. Several buildings were on fire.

11:00 pm: President Obama had a pre-scheduled meeting with Defense Secretary Leon Panetta, who told him of the attack and stated it was a coordinated terrorist attack.

12 September 2012

12:00 am: Tyrone Woods and his team arrived back at the CIA Annex, and soon thereafter came under attack by a well armed terrorist organization with mortars, RPGs, etc. It lasted almost until dawn, and they estimated that they killed about sixty of the Libyan attackers.

12:07 am: The State Department Operations Center received a report from the U.S. Embassy in Tripoli that the al-Qaeda extremist group, Ansar al-Sharia, had claimed responsibility for the Benghazi attack. No mention was ever made of any video issue.

1:30 am: Obama called and talked with Israeli Prime Minister Netanyahu for about an hour, trying to repair relations with him. Obama wanted to get the Jewish vote in the upcoming November election.

2:00 am: Ambassador Stevens was pronounced dead at a local hospital. Cause of death was listed as cardiac arrest, from smoke inhalation.

2:30 am: From this time on, no accounting has been made as to where President Obama was. He was scheduled for an early flight to Las Vegas, so he could attend a fund raiser. It was assumed he went to bed. The White House has never given an account for his time, after 2:30 am.

5:15 am: Tyrone Woods and Glen Doherty were killed in a mortar attack, as they tried to defend the CIA Annex. Doherty had just arrived from Tripoli, as part of a six man rescue team, when he was cut down by the mortar round.

<u>7:40 am:</u>   The Annex had been successfully evacuated and the first Americans had been flown out to Germany.

The Obama administration initially blamed the showing of a trailer on YouTube, publicizing a movie named "Innocence of Muslims" produced by a Nakoula Basseley Nakoula, as the reason the four Americans were killed in Benghazi. The truth was that Leon Panetta, the Secretary of Defense, had a meeting at 5:00 pm EDT with President Obama, in which he told the President the attack was a coordinated terrorist invasion of the Benghazi Mission (POST). However, the Obama administration continued to blame the video for several days after the deaths of the four Americans.

The blaming of the attack, on the video, fit the narrative the Obama administration was spreading, in the warm up to the November 2012 presidential election. Specifically, this narrative was that the Obama administration had eliminated Osama bin Laden, the al-Qaeda leader, on the 2nd of May 2011, and the terrorist organization was now on the ropes. Therefore, any mention of an organized attack, by al-Qaeda or any other terrorist group, was not encouraged by the administration. In fact, the claim that al-Qaeda was degraded was far from the truth.

On the 14th of September, President Obama and Secretary Clinton went to Dover AFB, for the ceremony to receive the bodies of the four Americans killed in Benghazi. Hillary Clinton, in her remarks, stated that she had received a communication from the

179

Palestinian Authority President Mahmoud Abbas praising Ambassador Stevens and deploring the ugly act of terror. President Abbas made no mention of the anti-Muslim video.

On the same day, the 14th, Leon Panetta went to Capitol Hill, to meet with the Senate Armed Services Committee about the attack. Based on his testimony, both the Republicans and the Democrats, on the committee, came away with the conclusion that the attack was a fully organized incursion, by well armed Islamic terrorists. Even Carl Levin, a Democrat and Chairman of the Senate Committee, stated that he thought it was a planned, premeditated attack.

However, four days later, on the 16th of September, U.S. Ambassador to the United Nations, Susan Rice, went on five television networks, blaming the Benghazi attack and deaths on an anti-Islamic video that was distributed on YouTube. She made no mention of coordinated attacks by radical Islamic extremists, such as Ansar al-Sharia. Again, her claim that the deaths were a result of the video fit the narrative the White House was trying to spin. On the same day, in direct contradiction to Rice, the new Libyan President, Mohamed Magariaf, stated on CBS News "Face the Nation" program that the attack on the U.S. Special Mission had been planned, well in advance.

Also on the same day, President Magariaf had an interview on National Public Radio (NPR), in which he is quoted as basically saying: The idea that this criminal and cowardly act was a spontaneous protest is just completely unfounded and preposterous. We believe it was a well planned, calculated mission to attack the U.S. consulate.

Towards the end of September, the three Americans killed in Benghazi, Sean Smith, Tyrone Woods and Glen Doherty were laid to rest in their home towns. Ambassador Stevens was buried at the family plot located in Grass Valley, California by the end of November, a little over two months after his death.

Congress started to hold hearings on the timing and cause of the tragedy in Benghazi. As is often the case, the investigation became very partisan, and there was considerable wrangling over the meetings, between Republicans who wanted to get the truth and the Democrats that were trying to protect the President and the Secretary of State.

Hillary Clinton was called to testify, but the meeting with Congress was delayed a few times, due to a supposed health issue. It is still debated as to whether she was delaying her testimony, or was really sick. Anyway, she recovered, and in January 2013, she did go before a Senate hearing on the Benghazi attack.

The 23rd of January 2013 Senate hearing was very contentious, and there was a heated exchange between Senator Ron Johnson of Wisconsin and the Secretary of State Hillary Clinton. In response to a question from Senator Johnson, Clinton said, with clenched teeth, in an irritated, challenging tone, "With all due respect, the fact is, we had four dead Americans! Was it because of a protest or was it because of guys out for a walk one night and decided they'd kill some Americans? **What difference, at this point, does it make?**"

Situation Analysis:

There are other questions that, when answered, may lead to the main answer, as to why the Special Mission (consulate) was attacked in the first place. The 11th of September 2012 was the eleventh anniversary of the 9/11 attack in New York. This could have some significance. If so, why wasn't the security at the Benghazi mission (called a POST by Obama) beefed up. The other obvious choice was to abandon it, until it was strengthened. There had been many attacks during the year 2012, aimed at Western facilities in the Benghazi area. This was a major **BLUNDER** on the part of the State Department, Secretary of State Hillary Clinton and the Obama administration. The security of the Benghazi facility was below State Department specifications, and only the Secretary of State could approve the use of the mission regardless, which she did.

In 2011, Hillary Clinton wanted to start a revolution in Libya, so she could claim she got rid of Gaddafi, during her tenure as Secretary of State. The Pentagon fought her on this, since the Joint Chiefs were smart enough to realize that the removal of the Gaddafi regime would leave a large power vacuum. This is what happened, and the Islamic extremists took advantage of it to spread their influence. Since Hillary Clinton wanted to leave the office of Secretary of State at the end of Obama's first term (whether he won reelection or not), she wanted to leave with the new Benghazi Consulate in place. She planned to visit Libya in December 2012 and announce the new diplomatic mission in Benghazi, the town where the revolution started. She believed this would be a feather in her cap.

One major question is why was Ambassador Stevens in Benghazi in the first place? There are rumors that he was there to facilitate the collection of weapons that the United States had given the Libyan opposition during the revolution. The U.S. wanted to collect as many weapons as possible, especially sophisticated ones like the Russian SA-7 Grail missiles, and ship them to the Syrian militants fighting Basher el-Assad's regime. The last meeting, by Stevens before he died, was with the Turkish Consul General Ali Sait Akin, to negotiate weapons transfer through Turkey to the Syrian opposition.

Russian MANPAD SA-7 Grail

On the 6th of September 2012, five days before the Benghazi attack, a ship named Al Entisar (Libya flagged) docked in the Turkish port of Iskenderun, just thirty five miles away from Syria. Shipping reports state that it was carrying 400 tons of cargo. Rumors

RICHARD OSBORN

are that the cargo was mainly RPGs, mortars, SA-7 anti-aircraft missiles (similar to the General Dynamics, Pomona designed Redeye and Stinger missiles) and ammunition.

Another question unanswered is why did the United States arm the militants, who had basically an al-Qaeda background, during the Libyan revolution in the first place? Did we not learn our mistake in Afghanistan, when we gave weapons to al-Qaeda, and later had to try and retrieve them? If you don't follow or read history, you are bound to make the same **BLUNDERS**.

Maybe Ambassador Stevens was in Benghazi to satisfy Hillary Clinton's desire to set up a permanent diplomatic mission in the city, where the revolution against Gaddafi started. According to a State Department spokeswoman, Ambassador Stevens was in Benghazi for diplomatic meetings, with who has never been clarified, and to attend the opening of a cultural center.

Any investigation into the Benghazi tragedy has yet to determine why Stevens was in the city to begin with. This might determine why the mission was attacked and destroyed. It would also ascertain, obviously, why Ambassador Stevens and the other three Americans were killed.

A more sinister reason for the attack might be that someone wanted Ambassador Christopher Stevens dead, to silence him because he knew too much. This would not be the first time, someone has been eliminated to stop them from talking.

On the other hand, the entire situation may have been one big **BLUNDER**. Inattention, by the people responsible for the diplomats and facilities, may have just caused a tragedy that resulted in four Americans losing their lives. In other words, it could also be called a dereliction of duty.

18

Syrian Civil War
2011 to Present

The country of Syria, known as Arab Levant, was carved out of the Ottoman Empire at the end of World War One, and France was given a mandate by the League of Nations to administer it. This mandate also included most of the area called Lebanon. The whole idea was developed two years before the end of WWI, when Sir Mark Sykes of Great Britain and Francois Georges Picot had a secret meeting. On the 19th of May 1916, they developed the secret accord that would basically divide up the Ottoman Empire.

There were three major Bedouin tribes near Syria's largest city, Damascus; Ruwalla, Fadl and the Hassana. From 1920 to 1946, France tried to control all the tribes in Syria and administer the country, until it became independent in April 1946, when the last French troops left. For the next fifty five years, Syria went through several troubling times with military coups. From 1958 to 1961, Syria joined Egypt in the United Arab Republic (UAR), which did not turn out very well for the Syrians. Egypt dominated the organization (country), and it ultimately broke up in September 1961, only three years after its formation.

In November of 1970, there was a major coup in Syria, and Hafez al-Assad came to power, ruling the country for the next thirty years. When he died in June 2000, his son Bashar al-Assad became President, and he is still running the country, as of the writing of this book.

On the 15th of March 2011, two hundred protesters gathered in Damascus to demand political and economic reforms, as well as the resignation of the Assad government. The Internet social media websites, such as Facebook and Twitter, were used to help organize the low attendance protests. The actual civil war, against the regime of Basher al-Assad's regime, began in the city of Daraa, close to the Syrian southern border with Jordan, on Tuesday the 17th of March 2011, also called "The Day of Rage".

What actually happened in Daraa, depends on which side you want to believe; the Syrian Government or the opposition dissidents. The dissidents' story is that Government troops came into Daraa in several trucks and shot many of the protesters. The Government claimed that the militants spread oil on the roads, and when the Government trucks skidded and crashed on the oily roads, they opened fire, killing numerous Syrian soldiers. Either way, the Syrian revolution against Assad's regime was under way. When word of what happened in Daraa got out, protests spread to other cities like Homs, Banyas and the suburbs of Damascus.

RICHARD OSBORN

Timeline of Events for Syrian Civil War

DATES	EVENTS
10 June 2000	President Hafez al-Assad died from a heart attack and his son Bashar succeeded him
17 July 2000	Bashar al-Assad was sworn in as president of Syria and Ba'ath party general secretary
6 September 2007	Syrian nuclear facility at al-Kibar was destroyed by Israel in Operation Orchard
26 January 2011	Protests started in Syria calling for political reforms and civil rights
15 March 2011	Syrian Day of Rage protests in support of the Arab spring took place
2 September 2011	European Union announced a ban of the import of Syrian oil
2 October 2011	Syrian opposition groups established the Syrian National Council
27 November 2011	Arab League voted to impose sanctions against Syria
6 February 2012	US closed its embassy in Damascus and recalled its diplomats
16 June 2012	United Nations suspended its monitoring mission due to intensifying violence
25 July 2012	International Committee of the Red Cross said fighting widespread and now Civil War
20 August 2012	Obama announced a red line which would be crossed if Syria used chemical weapons
3 December 2012	Obama said Assad should know there'd be consequences if he used chemical weapons
25 April 2013	Secretary of Defense Hagel stated US had evidence sarin gas had been used
30 August 2013	Secretary of State Kerry announced US had info 1429 Syrians killed by gas last week
4 September 2013	Obama stated that he did not set a red line, the world did, and he did nothing.
13 February 2014	It was announced that Syria had only shipped out 11% of its chemical stocks
29 June 2014	Islamic State was established with Abu Bakr al Baghdadi as caliph
19 August 2014	First American (James Foley) was executed by ISIS in the desert and broadcast on video
16 September 2014	ISIS started to attack the city of Kobani on the Syrian/Turkish border

In order to try and defuse the situation, President Assad announced the lifting of the State of Emergency, fired the entire current government and released some low level political prisoners. In May, Syrian armored vehicles entered Damascus, Homs, and Daraa, in an attempt to put down the uprisings. However, this only made matters worse. In June, the Government claimed over 100 soldiers had been killed by militants, in the northern town of Jisr al Shughour. Syrian troops attacked the rebels, and a considerable number of civilians fled across the border into Turkey, trying to avoid the violence.

In July, the various opposition groups met in Turkey in order to try and come up with a unified front, against President Assad. In the same month, the Syrian President removed the Hama province governor and sent in troops, to keep order. For the remainder of 2011, Syria saw violence spread across the entire nation, with a corresponding increase in destruction and deaths; civilians, soldiers and militants. Several top level Syrian military and political leaders deserted to the rebel side, and they assisted in the attacks, on the government positions.

By October 2011, the opposition had finally come to an agreement, and they formed the Syrian National Council. It was hoped this organization would present a united front against Assad and provide leadership, in the attacks on the government positions. By December, Syria had agreed to allow Arab League observers into the country, but they did not stay long. The observers left in January 2012, due to the increased violence and the associated danger to their staff.

By the beginning of 2012, the violence had turned into a full blown civil war, in which neither side seemed to be gaining the upper hand. In February, an attempt by Western powers to pass a draft resolution on Syria, in the United Nations Security Council, was vetoed by Russia and China. The UN estimated that the death toll so far in the Syrian civil war was around 7,500 civilians, with untold number of militants and soldiers. In June 2012, the Syrian civil war seemed to expand, when a Syrian jet shot down a Turkish plane. Turkey, in response, warned Syria that if any Syrian troops came close to the border, they would be viewed as a threat, and Turkey would act accordingly.

In July 2012, the Free Syrian Army (FSA) blew up some buildings in Damascus, killing some high ranking Syrian security officials, and at the same time it mounted a large scale attack on Aleppo, a key Syrian City in the northwest of the country. The Government tried to retake the city, but it could not make much headway. It was around this time that ISIS became one of the main militant organizations opposing Assad, and it started to attract many followers to its ranks.

By the beginning of July, the Syrian military began a renewed offensive on Aleppo and the town of Azaz. This attack went on until the 19th of July, when the FSA militants drove off the Syrian army and re-established control of Azaz. In the fighting, between seven and seventeen Syrian tanks were destroyed, mainly by RPGs. The number depended on who was making the claim. The rebel Tawhid Brigade was instrumental in the capture of Azaz, and they had received substantial weapon and ammunition support, via the Turkish border from unnamed Western powers. The success of the rebels seemed to have been affected by two reasons; increased supplies of weapons and training, and the reduced effectiveness of the fighting techniques by the Government's military.

Two Destroyed Syrian Tanks
Azaz, Syria August 2012
Photo by Christaan Triebert

On the 12th of August 2012, President Obama drew a red line about the use of chemical weapons by Syria, and in a response to a reporter's question, he stated, "I have, at this point, not ordered military engagement in the situation. But the point that you made about chemical and biological weapons is critical. That's an issue that doesn't just concern Syria; it concerns our close allies in the region, including Israel. It concerns us. We cannot have a situation where chemical or biological weapons are falling into the hands of the wrong people. We have been clear to the Assad regime, but also to other players on the ground, that a **red line for us** is we start seeing a whole bunch of chemical weapons moving around or being utilized. That would change my calculus. That would change my equation." This statement by Obama would come back to haunt him later, and he would try to change his words, by claiming the red line was not his, but the international community's line.

Tensions rose again in October, when five Turkish civilians were killed by Syrian mortar fire coming across the border, and Turkey returned the fire on the Syrians. In the same month, on Thursday the 11th of October, the Turks intercepted a Syrian passenger jet and forced it to land at Esenboga airport, in Ankara. It was carrying military arms from the Russian Federation to Syria, for use by the Syrian army. This incident raised tensions between Turkey and Syria, with Syria claiming the forced landing endangered the lives of the passengers and crew. The result was that both Syria and Turkey banned each other's aircraft, from their respective airspace.

On the 3rd of November 2012, three Syrian tanks entered the Golan Heights, and Israel complained to the UN peacekeepers about the incursion. Then, on the 11th of the month, Syria fired a mortar across the border, and the shell landed close to an Israeli army position. This was the second day in a row that this had happened. This time Israel returned fire with their tanks, and they aimed their fire at a Syrian artillery battery. Israel was concerned that Assad was targeting Israel deliberately, in order to draw international attention away, from what was happening in the Syrian civil war.

On the 31st of January 2013, Israeli aircraft attacked a convoy of trucks parked at a Syrian Research center in Jamraya, near Damascus. It was believed that the convoy was destined for Hezbollah in Lebanon, and that it contained sophisticated weapons and munitions, such as the Russian built SA-17 anti-aircraft missiles. It was reported that there were loud explosions after the attack, and that the planes also targeted an Iranian commander, who was accompanying the shipment to Hezbollah.

Note: The SA-17, also known as the BUK system, was the same anti-aircraft missile system that supposedly shot down MH17 over the Ukraine on the 17th of July 2014.

In April 2013, the United States and Britain demanded that the United Nations investigate reports of Syrian government forces using chemical weapons; meanwhile the civil war continued unabated. During this month, Prime Minister Wael Nader Al-Halqi narrowly escaped an assassination attempt, in the center of Damascus.

A United Nations June 2013 report declared there was reasonable proof that chemical weapons had been used in the civil war, but that there was not enough evidence to prove which side was the perpetrator, or what delivery system had been used. Some information, collected by U.S. Intelligence organizations, confirmed that the major rebel group al-Nusra had the ability to acquire and use chemical weapons. Maybe, they were using a false flag operation to shift blame for the attacks onto the Assad regime.

Then, on the 21st of August, there were reports of a sarin chemical attack by surface-to-surface rockets on militants and civilians in the Ghouta region, an area to the south and east of Damascus. The region consisted mainly of a collection of farms and agricultural plots. The death toll was estimated to be between 280 and 1,725, and both sides in the civil war blamed each other for the gas attack. The Russians blamed the attack on the opposition to President Assad, in a false flag operation.

In response to the attacks, the British Parliament voted against military action on the 30th of August 2013, while the U.S. Senate approved limited action in response to the chemical attack on the 4th of September. However, the Senate resolution specified that "boots on the ground" were not approved. In the end, even though the U.S. military was prepared to launch Tomahawk missiles, the order never came from the White House and the Commander-in-Chief.

Two weeks later, on the 14th of September 2013, the U.S. and Russia announced an agreement on the Framework of Syrian Chemical Weapons. Under this agreement, all chemical stocks would be collected and destroyed. In October 2013, the Syrian regime allowed United Nations inspectors to start the destruction of the chemical stocks, under the United States / Russian agreement.

At the end of 2013, Great Britain and the U.S. stopped shipping humanitarian goods to the rebels, because of reports that many of them were Islamic extremists. The beginning of 2014 saw an increase of activity by the more militant rebel groups, especially in the north and in Iraq. The border between Syria and Iraq was becoming very porous, and the rebels moved back and forth with ease.

In early 2014, peace talks between the Assad regime and the rebels broke down, mainly because the Bashar Assad would not agree to a transitional government. The year 2014 saw an improvement in the fortunes of the Assad regime. They recaptured various towns including Yabroud and Homs, although it was a hollow victory, since much of the towns had been destroyed.

In June 2014, the United Nations mission stated that the Syrian chemical stocks had been removed. The report also stated that all munitions, storage, mixing, production equipment had been destroyed. The same month, U.S Forces were landed on Iraq's Mount Sinjar, by a Bell Boeing Osprey V-22 aircraft, to coordinate the rescue and evacuation of some Yazidi refugees, trapped there by ISIS.

On the 30th of June 2014, the Islamic State (IS) was declared to be an Islamic caliphate and consisted of parts of Syria and Iraq. Abu Bakr al-Baghdadi was declared the Caliph of the Muslims. The territory that IS controlled stretched from Aleppo in the northwest of Syria through Iraq to Diyala. It was also declared that the term ISIS would no longer be used to describe their organization. Henceforth, Islamic State (IS) would be the official name for the group.

On the 24th of August 2014, Tabqa air force base, the last stronghold of the Syrian regime in the Raqqa province, fell to the IS, after heavy fighting and many casualties on each side. With the capture of this base, IS controlled the entire Raqqa province. IS also captured some MIG fighter planes and other equipment.

President Obama, on the 10th of September, announced in a speech that the United States would bomb certain targets in Syria, in order to degrade and halt the advance of IS. Following this speech, the U.S., Jordan and other Arab countries launched air attacks on IS positions in Syria, including those at Kobani that the IS was trying to capture from the Kurds. This speech was partially in response to the beheadings of the three Americans that started in June 2014.

As of the beginning of 2015, the Syrian civil war continues with no clear end in sight. IS seems to be getting stronger, although the U.S. bombing at Kobani has saved the town for now. Reports coming out of Syria seem to cast doubt on the total elimination of chemical stocks, storage facilities and chemical capability. Although much of it has been eliminated, the United Nations has not verified that chemical weapons, in Syria, have been completely destroyed.

After four years of civil war, Bashar al-Assad is still in power, with the assistance of Iran and Russia. As long as these two countries continue to support the Syrian dictator, he will probably remain as president.

Situation Analysis:

The events in the Syrian civil war and the lack of an effective U.S. response, has highlighted the deficiencies and the dearth of ideas, in the Obama/Clinton foreign policy. They didn't seem to know what to do, or how to coordinate an alliance to handle the situation. Maybe, they were and are still trying to **APPEASE** Russia and Iran, with whom they had ongoing negotiations about other matters (nuclear for one). Syria, in some ways, is a client state or satellite of Iran and the Russian Federation. Iran funnels arms through Syria to Hezbollah in Lebanon, and in addition there are many Iranian troops in Syria, helping Assad put down the revolt. With Syria's approval, Russia has a naval facility at the port of Tartus, located on the Syrian Mediterranean coast just north of Lebanon. Russia would hate to lose this facility, if Assad was overthrown. It is currently the only base Russia has in the Mediterranean Sea, although it is suspected that they are trying to negotiate a navy base in Egypt (see Chapter 22).

The Syrian uprising started almost on the same day, as the Libyan revolt. Why did Hillary Clinton push for the U.S. to support the Libyan rebels and topple the Gaddafi regime, while she did nothing about the Syrian revolution and help topple Assad? It appears that Obama, who had no coherent ideas of his own, left many aspects of foreign policy up to his Secretary of State and Valerie Jarrett, his principal advisor. The failure to provide an adequate response, to the Syrian uprising, was a major **BLUNDER** on the part of the Obama administration, and it may come back to haunt the President.

In January of 2014, President Obama gave an interview to the New Yorker magazine in which he stated that ISIS was a JV (Junior Varsity) team and of not real consequence, except in local power struggles. This pointed out Obama's misunderstanding of the threat posed by ISIS and other Islamic extremists. In fact, the Obama administration refuses to use the term "Islamic Extremists" to define the enemy. The reason for this is known only to President Obama. Since this interview to the New Yorker, ISIS, or IS, as it is now called, has advanced into many regions of Syria and Iraq. They are using terror, murder, robbery, oil sales and other nefarious methods, to expand their forces and territory. They are also killing Christians, just because of their religion, and the U.S. government, up to now, has not shown much remorse.

IS is seen as a competitor, and also as a partner to al-Qaeda. In some situations, they cooperate in terrorist operations, as IS does with other militant organizations, around the world. As of now, Yemen seems to be falling apart, and IS can be expected to try and expand their reach into this Gulf of Aden nation.

On the 12th of August 2012, President Obama had never read or he had forgotten the following paraphrased advice, given to the world by Napoleon Bonaparte. "If you state you are going to take Vienna, TAKE VIENNA". Obama drew a red line about the use or transport of chemical weapons by Syria. When it actually happened, Obama **APPEASED** Assad by stating that he meant the international community had drawn the line, not him. This excuse was rubbish or TOSH, as some people call it.   Any President should know, if you state you are going to do something, that you do it, or you lose credibility.

You can bet Russia and Iran made note of this **APPEASEMENT** and they will act accordingly in the Ukraine issue, and the nuclear negotiations. Please read chapters twenty for the Iran situation, with the nuclear deliberations between them and the US, and chapter twenty-one for the desire by Putin to take over part or all of the Ukraine.

19

Afghanistan
2001 to 2014

Down through history, Afghanistan has been legendary, as the crossroads between the Middle East and Asia. Many invaders have passed through the country, including Darius, Alexander the Great and Genghis Khan. The Khyber Pass is the main route from Afghanistan to Pakistan, and for many years, it was controlled by the British, during the heyday of the British Empire.

In 1920, two years after World War One, the British decided to build a railway through the Pass for strategic reasons. At that time, they controlled much of Pakistan and India, and they needed good communications and transportation facilities through Afghanistan. The first train puffed its way through the Pass, on the 4th of November 1925, five years after the construction was started.

On the 8th of November 1933, Mohammed Zahir Shah became King of Afghanistan at the age of nineteen, on the assassination of his father, and he remained the ruler, until the monarchy was overthrown in 1973. Mahommed Daoud Khan took over as President of the new republic of Afghanistan, and remained in the office, until he was assassinated in 1978, during a Communist takeover of the country. For the next twenty-four years, the country went through a series of leaders and infighting.

In December 1979, the Soviet Union, under orders from Leonid Brezhnev, invaded Afghanistan and tried to control it, with its army and air force, for nine long years. Russia had a long history of trying to influence events in the country, in the 18th and 19th centuries. The war cost thousands of lives of Russian soldiers, and many Afghanistan soldiers also died. At the peak of its occupation, the Soviets had a force of 115,000 soldiers and airmen in the country. Mainly, they remained in the valleys, as the mountains were too dangerous for them. They used helicopter gunships to strafe villages, and they indiscriminately killed women and children, as well as men. The United States supplied arms and shoulder launched Stinger missiles to the Mujahideen resistance fighters, who became very effective in shooting down Soviet aircraft and helicopters.

Finally, in February 1989, Mikhail Gorbachev, the last General Secretary of the Soviet Union, withdrew the remaining troops out of the country. During the entire campaign, approximately 14,400 Russians were killed and 53, 750 wounded. The war was referred to as the Soviet Union's Vietnam War, with the casualties and no victory. From 1989 to 2001, Afghanistan went through some troubling times, with Al-Qaeda training camps being set up, and the Taliban running the country.

Timeline of Events in Afghan Emergency

DATES	EVENTS
11 September 2001	Al-Qaeda terrorists attacked the New York twin towers with fueled commercial aircraft
7 October 2001	United States and United Kingdom attacked Afghanistan in support of Northern Alliance
12 November 2001	Talban forces abandoned Kabul under the onslaught of the US and Northern Alliance
11 August 2003	NATO officially took command of the peacekeeping in Afghanistan
9 August 2004	Hamid Karzai won, by 55.4% of the vote, the Afghanistan presidential election
6 April 2005	Chinook helicopter crashed in dust storm killing 15 US troops and 3 civilians
17 June 2007	Taliban suicide bomber blew up Afghan police bus killing 35
7 July 2008	Suicide bomber attacked Indian embassy and killed more than fifty
9 September 2008	President Bush sent 4,500 extra troops in a "quiet surge" to help quell violence
1 December 2009	Obama announced 30,000 additional troops (surge) for a total of 100,000 troops
17 January 2010	Kabul's Day of Terror – gun battles near the Afghanistan Presidential Palace
23 June 2010	General Petraeus was nominated to take over as commanding general in Afghanistan
18 September 2010	Afghan Parliamentary elections were held but criticized as fraudulent
26 January 2011	The Afghan National Assembly was inaugurated, most members are war lords
2 May 2011	Osama bin Laden, head and founder of al-Qaeda, was killed in Pakistan by US forces
6 August 2011	31 American special forces killed when their helicopter crashed-probably shot down
25 May 2012	French President Hollande says France would withdraw troops by end of 2012
18 June 2013	Afghan army took command of all military and security from NATO
29 September 2014	Ashraf Ghani was sworn in as President after a controversial presidential election
26 October 2014	US and UK ceased combat operations in Afghanistan

The Taliban seized control of Kabul, on the 27th of September 1996, and changed the government, to a harsh Islamic type of justice. Then in August of 1998, President Clinton authorized missile strikes on the al-Qaeda training camps, in response to the bomb attacks on U.S. Embassies in Tanzania and Kenya. Ahmad Shah Masood, an influential leader of the Northern Alliance in Afghanistan, was assassinated by a double agent, and his death eliminated a major, potential threat to the Taliban

All this came to a head on the 11th of September 2001, when the New York twin towers were destroyed, by two hijacked, commercial jet liners. Immediately, President George W. Bush asked Congress for approval to use military force. The resolution was approved on the 14th of September 2001 and signed by Bush, a few days later. On the 7th of October, the United States initiated Operation Enduring Freedom, with bombs raining down on the Taliban and the al-Qaeda forces. The Northern Alliance joined in the fighting, and it soon captured Kabul, with American military assistance.

In December 2001, Hamid Karzai was sworn in as the provisional President of Afghanistan, and in January 2002, NATO deployed its first peacekeepers, in an organization known as ISAF (International Security Assistance Force). Then in April 2002, the former king of the country, Mohammed Zahir Shah, returned to Kabul, but he did not make any claims to the throne. He just wanted to return to his country, and he died there five years later.

On the 11th of August 2003, NATO/ISAF took responsibility for security control of Kabul. Five months later, in January 2004, Afghanistan adopted a new constitution that specified the country would have a strong president. In the fall of 2004, Hamid Karzai was elected President for the first time, and he was sworn in on the 4th of December 2004. Parliamentary elections also took place on the 18th of September 2005, and the people voted for the first time in over thirty years.

NATO/ISAF took over security control, from the United States, for the entire country, on the 5th of October 2006. This would turn out to be a challenge, because the violence did not go away. The Taliban continued sporadically to bomb buildings and assassinate politicians. The Islamic extremists attacked the Indian Embassy, in Kabul, with a suicide bomber on the 7th of July 2008, in which more than forty-one people were killed.

In September of 2008, President Bush initiated a "quiet surge" in which 4,000 to 5,000 marines and army personnel were reassigned to Afghanistan. In January 2009, President Bush left office and Barack Hussein Obama was sworn in as the new President. One month later, President Obama announced that an additional 17,000 troops would go to Afghanistan, and NATO pledged additional troops in support of the new surge. This was a complete reversal by Obama, who was against the earlier surge in Iraq. On the 2nd of December 2009, Obama increased the number of troops again by 30,000, bringing the total up to around 100,000. As he made this announcement, he stated that he would start the withdrawal of forces by the end of 2011.

Violence continued unabated throughout the country, with the Taliban being the main culprit. An Al-Qaeda double agent named Humam Khalil Abu-Mulai al-Balawi, a doctor from Jordan, donned a suicide vest and walked into Camp Chapman, near Khost, and blew himself up. It turned out he was a dedicated Islamist extremist, but the CIA thought he was on their side and seven CIA agents ended up dead.

In February 2010, NATO forces started a major offensive, named Operation Moshtarak, that targeted the Helmand Province, and in particular the town of Marjah. This province was a major stronghold of the Taliban Islamic extremists. The operation commenced on the 13th of February 2010 and it continued, off and on, for ten months ending on the 7th of December.

UH-60 Black Hawk Helicopter in Marjah
evacuating wounded U.S. Marines

Initially the operation was somewhat successful, but the Afghans were not able to set up an administration in the Marjah to counter the Taliban. By May 2010, three months into the mission, U.S. General Stanley McChrystal referred to it as a "bleeding ulcer", and it continued to be a problem for the troops, until operation Moshtarak was declared officially over in December.

On the 10th of August 2010, the Dutch 2,000 troop contingent called it quits, and they headed for home, after a four year mission in Afghanistan, as part of NATO. Dutch leaders earlier that year had said that the troops would be brought home in 2010. The removal of the Dutch troops cast some doubt on the viability of the entire NATO mission in the country. In September of the same year, parliamentary elections, that took place under extreme violence, were marred by claims of fraud and delays, in announcing who won.

At the beginning of 2011, President Karzai made an official visit to the Russian Federation, the first since the USSR pulled its troops out of Afghanistan in 1989. On Friday the 1st of April, seven United Nations workers and seven other foreigners were killed in Kabul violence, triggered by the burning of the Koran by a Florida pastor. Four of the men killed were from Nepal, and the other three foreigners were from Europe.

On the 25th of April 2011, approximately five hundred Taliban prisoners broke out of a prison in Kandahar, by digging a one thousand foot tunnel. It took the prisoners five months to dig the tunnel, during the winter months.

President Karzai's half brother and Kandahar governor, Ahmad Wali Karzai, was assassinated on the 12th of July, during a Taliban campaign against prominent political figures. Two months later on the 20th of September, a former president of Afghanistan from 1992-1996, Burhanuddin Rabbani, was killed by a suicide bomber. The assassin, dressed as a normal Afghan citizen, came up to Rabbani, hugged him in friendship and then blew himself up.

The violence continued by both sides through the rest of 2011. On the 26th of November, a NATO airstrike killed several Pakistan soldiers on the border, in a friendly fire accident, which caused the Pakistan government to stop the movement of NATO trucks through the country, for nearly six months. On the 6th of December, more than fifty-eight civilians were killed in two attacks on Shiite mosques; a suicide bomb in Kabul and a bicycle bomb in Mazat-i-Sharif.

On the 22nd of February 2012, copies of the Koran were burned at the US Bagram airbase, setting off five days of protests by the Afghans. The Korans were burned because officials believe they were being used to smuggle messages. In the violence that followed, thirty people, including four Americans, were killed, and the Taliban used the incident to incite riots in other areas of Afghanistan. As part of their spring offensive, the Taliban staged multiple attacks on the 15th of April 2012, using bombs, gunfire and rockets. The targets were foreign facilities and some government buildings, and the attacks were blamed by the government on the Haqqani network. In the end, the government forces killed thirty-eight of the attackers.

Arsala Rahmani Daulat, a former Taliban leader and a person very useful in trying to negotiate with the terrorist organization, was shot dead in his car on the 31st of May 2012. No organization claimed responsibility, but it did stall the talks between the Karzai government and the Taliban. On the 2nd of September, the United States temporarily suspended new police recruit training, due to security concerns and the danger of false flag operations. The U.S. wanted to make sure all the recruits had no ties with the Taliban.

In the same year, the United States handed over to the Afghanistan government most of the Parwan Detention Facility (Bagram High Security Jail), on the 10th of September. America did keep control over certain foreign prisoners until the 25th of March 2013, after which the entire facility was in Afghan hands.

The violence continued into 2013, but it seemed at a lower level. Perhaps the Taliban were biding their time, until the U.S. and NATO totally pulled out of the combat roll.

On the 5th of March 2013, the Kabul Bank chairman and chief executive respectively, Sherkhan Farnood and Khalilullah Ferozi, were jailed for major fraud that almost led to the collapse of the entire Afghanistan banking system in 2010. Then, on the 18th of June, the Afghan army took over, all combat and security rolls, from NATO and the United States. President Karzai delayed signing the new security agreement with the U.S., and he left it up to the new president to be elected the following year.

On the 18th of January 2014, the Taliban attacked a restaurant in Kabul's diplomatic area, with suicide bombers, and they killed thirteen foreigners, including the International Monetary Fund country head. Just two days later, on the 20th, seven bombers wearing ISAF uniforms, in a false flag operation, attacked an Afghan/ISAF base in Kandahar. All the attackers were shot, but not before two civilians and one NATO soldier were killed. No U.S. soldiers were killed in this attack.

During the year of 2014, these types of attacks continued, and in June, more than fifty civilians were killed during the second round of elections to select a new president. The Taliban was attempting to delay the election and cause any chaos they could. The election ended up inconclusive, with the sides of both major candidates claiming fraud. Finally, Ashraf Ghani was sworn in as President on the 29th of September 2014.

On the 1st of October 2014, the U.S., NATO and the Afghan government signed an agreement that allowed the stationing of troops in the country, after the end of 2014. These forces would be used mainly for training and security; no combat roles would be involved. The U.S. was planning to leave around 9,800 troops in the country, while all the others would be withdrawn under the agreement. On the 26th of October 2014, the U.S. and NATO troops hauled down their respective flags, and they ended combat operations in Afghanistan.

On the 28th of January 2015, the Obama White House labeled the Taliban as an "Armed Insurgency" and not a terrorist group. This definition allowed the Administration to "legally" trade Sergeant Bowe Bergdhal for five hardened Islamist extremists, held at Camp Guantanamo Bay. The U.S. officially does not negotiate with terrorists, but by calling it an Armed Insurgency, the White House claimed it did not trade hostages.

On Thursday the 29th of January 2015, three American contractors and an Afghan national were shot to death, at Kabul International Airport. The killer was dressed in an Afghan police uniform, in an apparent false flag operation. Even though the White House claims the war against the Taliban is over, it continues, and the Taliban can be expected to start a new spring offensive, around April 2015.

Situation Analysis:

The Afghanistan undeclared war lasted thirteen long years, before the United States pulled its combat troops out of the country. This was the longest "war" the U.S. has fought in, and we left without declaring victory. The Taliban are still there and will soon be back created more trouble, once the winter snows have melted. During the thirteen years, the United States suffered 2,257 soldiers killed and 19,950 wounded, and our coalition partners also suffered casualties.

The Obama administration announced well in advance when the U.S. would pull out, which allowed the Taliban the opportunity to plan accordingly. This will turn out to be a major **BLUNDER** on the part of the President and Commander-in-Chief. We would not have told Nazi Germany or Japan when we would end the war, so why did we do so in Afghanistan?

With the January 2015 attacks at Kabul airport, the Taliban showed that it is ready to continue the struggle. IS, Al-Qaeda and the Taliban can be expected to cooperate in some way once the spring offensive starts. We also **APPEASED** the Taliban by consenting to the swap of five key Taliban "generals" at Camp Justice in Guantanamo Bay, for one American deserter. This was a show of weakness by the Obama administration and the United States government, and you can bet all of America's enemies paid attention. These five Taliban Islamic terrorists can be expected to return to the fight, once their year of house arrest in Qatar is over, in May 2015. Already one has been caught contacting the Taliban in Afghanistan.

Just as chaos and violence reared its ugly head in Iraq once we pulled our troops out, so it is fairly safe to assume that the same situation will occur in Afghanistan. The ideology of the Islamic terrorists is very attractive to young men of the country, without much hope of getting any decent type of job, to earn a living. It is predicted that the drug trade will flourish, when the poppy fields start to grow in the next few months. We can anticipate that there will be more suicide bombings, targeting the political leaders of the government, which will cause a power vacuum into which the Taliban can move.

Iran, which is a neighbor of Afghanistan, can be expected to make some moves to try and influence events in the country, as they have in Yemen, Iraq, Syria and Lebanon. Iran's goal is to be the dominant power in the Middle East (see the next chapter) by using terrorism to cower the populations and to building a nuclear weapon, with which to threaten their neighbors.

On the 4th of February 2015, it was reported that the U.S. and Iran were getting close to a deal concerning Iran's nuclear program. Reportedly, the U.S. will allow Iran to keep running its centrifuges in exchange for their help in trying to stabilize the countries around them, including Afghanistan, Iraq and Syria. In addition, the U.S. would lift most, if not all, of the economic sanctions.

If this is true, it would represent a major **APPEASEMENT** by Obama that would rival the appeasement of Hitler by Chamberlain in 1938. The United States cannot trust the Iranians, any more than the British should have trusted Hitler. Iran's goal is to destroy Israel and become the master of the Middle East, with control of the oil wealth.

The next day, the 5th of February, the Principal Deputy under Secretary of Defense for Policy admitted before the Senate Armed Services Committee that the U.S. is "not at the end of hostilities in Afghanistan". The U.S. is allowed to fly missions in support of the Afghan army, which will probably resort in civilian deaths. This will allow the Taliban to create propaganda blasting the U.S. warmongers.

20

Iran – Nuclear and Missile Developments
2013/2014

Iran's hunt for nuclear technology began in 1987, towards the end of the Iran/Iraq war. A secret meeting was held between a German engineer, named Heinz Mebus, a Sri Lanka businessman, named Mohamed Farouqand, and three Iranian officials. The purpose of the meeting was to discuss an offer, by a Dr. Abdul Quadeer Khan of the Pakistan Kahuta Research Labs, to provide nuclear technology to Iran. Dr. Khan is considered the father of the Pakistan atomic bomb.

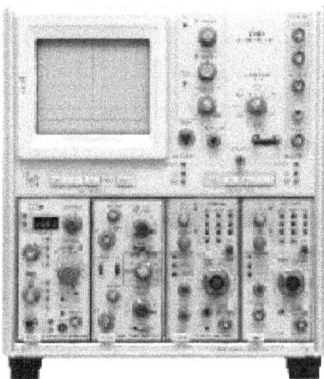

Tektronix , Inc.
Oscilloscope
Model 7904
500 MHz.

During the seventies and eighties, several U.S. companies, such as Tektronix Inc. and Hewlett-Packard, sold sophisticated electronic equipment to Pakistan, even though the United States knew it was going to be used in the development of nuclear weapons. The Tektronix, Inc. distributor sales manager covering Pakistan, in the 1970s, has confirmed that he visited the Pakistan nuclear laboratories for the purpose of promoting electronic equipment to its personnel. Actually, the Mossad, the Israeli Secret Service, had tried in 1981, but failed, to eliminate the German, Heinz Mebus, as they recognized him as being a threat to Israel.

Pakistan was not economically well off, so this opportunity to sell nuclear technology to Iran came in very useful. To Iran, it was a quicker way to become a nuclear power in the Middle East, and counter the influence of the Great Satan – the United States. In March of 1996, approximately six hundred Russian engineers started working on the Iranian Bushehr nuclear plant that was of an old, Russian design. Six years later, in September 2002, the Russians started building the actual nuclear reactor at Bushehr, despite strong protests from President Bush's administration.

In September 2003, the United Nations IAEA (International Atomic Energy Agency) gave Iran a few weeks, to prove it was not developing atomic weapons. In November of the same year, the Iranian government stated that they were suspending their uranium enrichment program, and would allow an inspection by the IAEA. After the IAEA inspected

Iran's nuclear facilities, they decided that Tehran was not pursuing nuclear weapons.

Six months later, on the 18th of June 2004, the IAEA chastised Iran, for failing to assist the Agency in its investigation of Iran's nuclear developments. On Sunday the 14th of November, Iran again agreed to suspend enrichment of uranium, in a deal with the European Union.

On the 8th of August 2005, Iran announced that they had resumed converting uranium at their Isfahan facility, and they stated it was for peaceful purposes. The IAEA accused Iran of violating the 1970 UN Non-Proliferation Treaty. In retaliation, Iran broke the United Nations IAEA seals on its Natanz nuclear plant on the 10th of January 2006, and in the beginning of February, it began again to enrich uranium, at Natanz. The IAEA voted 27-3 to report Iran's violations to the United Nations Security Council on the 4th of February. By April the 10th, Iran had succeeded in enriching uranium, according to its government.

The United Nations set a 31st of August deadline for Iran to suspend enrichment. The date passed, and the IAEA confirmed that Tehran had not ceased enriching uranium. In response to Iran's enrichment program, the UN voted, on the 23rd of December 2006, to impose sanctions on Iran's trade in nuclear technology. Iran condemned the UN resolution, and officials said they would continue to enrich uranium.

The year 2007 saw more of the same, with Iran ignoring the UN's call to suspend enrichment. The Iranian religious leaders actually were in no hurry to develop an atomic weapon, since they also needed a delivery system, in order to make it a threat to its neighbors and Europe. They were working on a long range rocket, with the North Korean's help, and were disguising its development, as a satellite launch vehicle.

On the 2nd of February 2007, the IAEA reported that Iran had failed to meet the latest deadline, for stopping enrichment. On the 24th of March, the UN Security Council voted to impose new economic and weapon sanctions on Iran, for its failure to cease enriching uranium. At the same time in March 2007, there was a major military engagement in the waters off Iran, when fifteen British sailors were detained by Iran, in international waters.

In April of that year, the President of Iran announced that they had 3,000 centrifuges in operation, and they were producing nuclear fuel on a large scale. On the 23rd of May 2007, the IAEA said Iran had enriched enough uranium that they could produce an atomic bomb in three to eight years. In July 2007, the IAEA was told by the Iranians that they could visit the Arak nuclear plant, if they wanted to.

Arak IR-40 Heavy Water Reactor

Source: Nanking 2012

TWILIGHT FOR THE WEST?

Timeline of Events in Iran Nuclear Program

DATES	EVENTS
3 December 1979	Ayatollah Khomeini became the Supreme Leader of Iran
19 January 1984	The U.S. added Iran to the list of states that sponsor terrorism
1987 to 1989	Iran obtained technical specifications to build a P-1 centrifuge from Pakistan
5 August 1996	U.S. passed the Iran Sanctions Act that penalized any major U.S. energy investment
August 2002	Information was passed on to the U.S. that Iran had built nuclear facility near Natanz
21 October 2003	Iran agreed to suspend its uranium enrichment with European foreign ministers
18 June 2004	The IAEA called out Iran for failure to halt enrichment and cooperate with its inspectors
8 August 2005	Iran began producing uranium hexafluoride at its Isfahan facility
1 June 2006	P5+1 proposed long term agreement similar to Europe's 8 Aug 2005 proposal
24 March 2007	UN Security Council passed 3rd resolution banning Iran from exporting arms
3 March 2008	UN Security Council passed 4th resolution tightening limits on Iran's nuclear activities
3 February 2009	Iran announced successful launch of a satellite with a long range missile
25 September 2009	US announced that Iran had built a secret, 2nd uranium enrichment facility at Fordo
21 August 2010	Iran obtained nuclear rods from Russia (by previous agreement) to run their reactor
10 May 2011	Iran announced that its Bushehr nuclear power plant began operation at a low level
10 January 2012	Iran announced it was enriching uranium at its Fordo facility near Qom
7 March 2013	The U.S. and Iran began secret talks in Oman that were not announced until later
23 November 2013	Talks between Iran and P5+1 break down and are extended until 23 July 2014
19 June 2014	Talks between Iran and P5+1 break down and are extended until 24 November 2014
24 November 2014	Talks between Iran and P5+1 break down and are extended until 1 July 2015

The Bush administration announced in October 2007 that the U.S. was imposing new sanctions against Iran, for violating international nuclear energy agreements. Three months later on the 3rd of December, the U.S. issued a new intelligence report on Iran, downplaying the threat that Iran posed in its nuclear weapons capability.

In February 2008, the Iranians launched a new type of rocket, to show the world that they were developing satellite launch capability. They did not mention that it might also be used to carry atomic bombs to targets in the Middle East, including Israel. In May of 2008, the IAEA accused Iran of withholding details of its nuclear program and notified the UN.

On the 9th of July 2008, Iran successfully launched the latest version of a long range missile, the Shahab-3, which would be able to hit most targets in the Middle East. Then, in August, they launched another rocket that could lift a satellite into earth's orbit. In September of the same year, the UN tried to impose new sanctions on Iran, but Russia refused to go along, threatening to use their veto power.

On the 3rd of February 2009, Iran finally succeeded in launching a satellite into orbit, atop the Shahab-3 rocket. Later, on the 20th of May of the same year, Iran launched a medium range, solid fuel missile, capable of reaching most of the Middle East, including Israel and U.S bases in the region. In June of 2009, there were riots in the streets of Tehran after that year's presidential election, when the government of Mahmoud Ahmadinejad was accused of rigging the election. The demonstrations were put down with force by the government and many demonstrators were arrested, with some ending up being executed.

Iran admitted, on the 21st of September 2009, that it was building a new enrichment facility in the town of Qom (about 80 miles south of Tehran), but claimed it was only for peaceful purposes. The same month, Iran again test fired several medium and long range rockets, and they placed a video on television, to show their unconfirmed capability. On the 29th of November, Iran announced they would be constructing ten more uranium enrichment plants, and at the same time turned down an offer, by UN Security Council members, to enrich uranium for Iran overseas.

In May 2010, Iran agreed to send uranium abroad for enrichment, but it did not state that it would cease enrichment in Iran itself. The Western powers were skeptical about this entire offer, and viewed it as more foot dragging by the Iranians. On the 9th of June, the UN imposed the fourth round of sanctions on Iran, and they included tightening the already imposed economic and weapons embargos. On the 10th of August, Iran, with the assistance of the Russians, started to load fuel rods into its Bushehr nuclear energy plant, and by the 26th of October, this loading was completed.

In September of 2010, a computer worm called Stuxnet had been detected in Bushehr and other Iranian nuclear facilities. Rumors abounded that Israel and/or the United States were involved, however no one claimed responsibility. Nuclear talks, between Iran and the West, started in Geneva on the 6th of December and ended the next day. They went nowhere, but both sides agreed to meet again in Istanbul, Turkey the next month.

The next round of talks started on the 21st of January 2011 in Istanbul, and again like the last meeting, they only lasted one day, until the 22nd. The talks failed and were adjourned, because Iran came to the meeting, with two major preconditions. The first prerequisite was that the sanctions on Iran must be lifted immediately, which the West would not accept. The second precondition was that the West must recognize Iran's right to enrich uranium. Again, the West would not accept this outright.

On the 10th of May 2011, Iran announced that the power generating equipment at Bushehr had started operating at a low level, and by the 3rd of September, the plant, running at full power, was connected to the Iranian power grid. The IAEA announced on the 8th of November 2011 that they had found evidence the Iranians had carried out research, on the development of a trigger device for a nuclear weapon.

On the 23rd of January 2012, the United States extended its sanctions on Iran to include its banking system that was a clearing house of profits, made in the sale of their oil. In the same month, the Iranians began enriching uranium, at its new Fordo facility. On February the 9th, the IAEA left Iran, after it was denied access to a new nuclear site at Parchin.

In the middle of May 2012, the West held nuclear talks with Iran that ended up again in a deadlock. On the 25th of May, the IAEA inspectors found evidence of uranium being enriched to 27% at the Fordo facility. On the 1st of July, the EU finally extended its boycott, to cover the import of oil from Iran or the import of Iranian oil from a third country. In September, the United Nations IAEA report, which is issued quarterly, indicated Iran had increased the production at Fordo two times, and that the IAEA had been denied access to the Parchin site.

The European Countries placed further sanctions on Iran, on the 16th of October 2012, and the next month, on the 16th of November, an IAEA report stated that Iran was capable of doubling its output of enriched uranium at the Fordo facility, as it had installed over 2700 centrifuges there.

In January 2013, Iran wrote a letter, dated the 23rd, which announced Iran was planning to upgrade its enrichment centrifuges, at the Natanz facility. These new devices would allow Iran to refine its uranium, at a quicker rate than before. Then, on the 9th of April 2013, Iran stated it had started operating two uranium mines, and a plant to process the ore from these mines. This would allow Iran to increase its capability in producing nuclear material for its facilities.

On the 24th of November 2013, there was an interim agreement between Iran and the Western powers (P5+1= U.S., Russia, China, UK, France and Germany) in Geneva. As a reward, the West agreed to relieve Iran of some $7B of the sanctions. In return, Iran agreed to give IAEA inspectors better access to facilities and to curb enrichment of uranium above the 5% limit. This agreement was to be implemented one month later, on the 20th of January 2014. It was also agreed that the next talks between

Iran and the P5+1 would take place in Vienna, Austria, on the 17th of March 2014. The talks lasted three days, but nothing much was accomplished, other than agreement to meet again in July.

In April 2014, the IAEA announced that Iran had neutralized about half of its highly-enriched uranium, as agreed to in Geneva, back on the 24th of November 2013. The next meeting (4th round) was scheduled for the 13th of May 2014, in Vienna. Nothing much was accomplished there and several more rounds of talks took place, over the next few months, as listed below:

Round	Date	Location
5th	16 June 2014	Vienna
6th	2 July 2014	Vienna
7th	19 Sept. 2014	New York
8th	16 Oct. 2014	Vienna
9th	11 Nov. 2014	Muscat, Oman
10th	18 Nov. 2014	Vienna
11th	17 Dec. 2014	Geneva
12th	18 Jan. 2015	Geneva

The 24th of November meeting, between Iran and the P5+1, became deadlocked over sanctions, the level of enrichment permitted and the number of centrifuges allowed. Coming out of this meeting, there was an interim agreement that the talks would be extended to the 1st of March 2015. This date was set as a deadline to reach a political framework agreement, and the date of the 1st of July 2015 for a final agreement, with all details being settled. In return for Iran agreeing to extend the talks, the United

States agreed, at the November 24th meeting, to release $700 million in frozen assets each month.

Situation Analysis:

The way, the P5+1 have negotiated with Iran over its nuclear program, is a massive example of **APPEASEMENT**. Iran has delayed, delayed and delayed, while the United States has lifted sanctions, hoping to **APPEASE** Iran and have them sign an agreement; any agreement. Any first grader could see why it would be to Iran's advantage to stall.

Iran is attempting to delay any requirement for shutting down or reducing their nuclear program, so they have time to develop a missile which can at least reach most of Europe. They are fast reaching that objective, and since their atomic bomb program is well advanced, it would not take much time to finish it and mount it on one missile.

All they need is one missile, with an atomic weapon mounted in a nose cone, to threaten their Middle East neighbors. In the meantime, the Obama administration has no strategy, to prevent Iran from achieving their goal.

In 2012, President Obama stated several times that he would not allow Iran to obtain the bomb. For example, on the 25th of September 2012, he stated in a speech at the United Nations, "Make no mistake: A nuclear armed Iran is not a challenge that can be contained....the United States will do what we must to prevent Iran from obtaining a nuclear weapon." However, the question is whether Obama meant it or was just saying it, because he was running for reelection, one month later. It was probably just words, just like the time he stated there was a red line in Syria over the use, or transportation, of chemical weapons.

One can only wonder what President Obama and advisor Valerie Jarrett's plans are for the United States. Valerie Jarrett was born in Shiraz, Iran and lived there for five plus years. One can only speculate as to whether she was indoctrinated in the Muslim faith, when she was educated there. President Obama was indoctrinated for many years as he sat and listened to Reverend Wright spew out his hatred, for the United States and the old colonial powers. Does the President, or his advisor, want Iran to obtain the "bomb"?

Is the "bomb" like the old six-shooter in the west? Does the President view the bomb as an equalizer just like the old six-shooter was?

The nuclear negotiations with Iran, first by the Europeans and now by the P5+1, have been going on for at least ten long years. How long does it take to decide if there will be an agreement or not?

As of today, it appears the negotiations have a long way to go. What will the United States do if no agreement is reached, by the 1st of July 2015? Will Obama and Kerry agree to extend the talks; if so, for how long? As it has been stated many times, it only took four years with the Manhattan project to develop the U.S. atomic weapon, and yet we can't seem to decide if Iran is serious, or not, in the negotiations.

Perhaps the best way, to prevent Iran getting the bomb, is by regime change. There are many exiles from Persia (Iran), some of whom would probably be willing to return, if supported by the U.S. as there were French resistance fighters, during World War Two. Is the United States broadcasting radio and television into Iran, just as VOA broadcast radio into Eastern Europe years ago? As far as it can be determined, the answer is a loud, resounding **NO**.

By the 1st of July 2015, we and the world will know, if Iran is serious in negotiating or just delaying, until they have the bomb and the missile. Of course, if the answer is no, and they are not serious in negotiating, it may be too late to put the genie back in the bottle.

There seems to be a plan afoot by the Obama administration, to take any agreement to the United Nations for approval. This would bypass the U.S. Senate, which under the constitution, has the duty to study, investigate and vote on any treaty, agreed to by the executive branch of the government. If President Obama and Secretary of State Kerry did this, it would be a **BLUNDER**, of the first order, that could poison the "well" in Washington for some time to come.

21

Ukraine/Crimea
2014

Down through the centuries, the Ukraine has been invaded, conquered, divided up and then put back together again. Towards the end of World War One, there was a war of independence, after the Russian Empire collapsed into chaos, with the arrival of Lenin. The Ukraine declared its independence on the 26th of January 1918, but the country's independence only lasted for three years. In 1921, the Ukraine, consisting of the Ukrainian People's Republic and the West Ukrainian People's Republic, became a founding member of the Soviet Union. Other territories were later added to the Ukraine, as a result of the German-Russian Non-Aggression Pact of August 1939.

During the early Stalin years, a great famine was created by the dictator, as a method of control, and millions of Ukrainians starved to death. The country is considered a "bread basket", due to the amount of grain that is grown there. During World War Two, Ukrainians picked sides, some going with the Germans, some with the Soviets and some on neither side. The Ukraine suffered greatly during and just after the war, as the Germans and then Stalin massacred thousands of the civilians.

After World War Two, the Constitution of the Ukraine Socialist Republic was amended, and it permitted the country to act somewhat independently. The Ukraine had its own vote in the United Nations, although it always voted with the USSR. On the 19th of February 1954, a decree was introduced and adopted by the Presidium of the Supreme Soviet of the Soviet Union, under Nikita Khrushchev, that transferred the Crimea Oblast to the Ukraine. This was a symbolic gesture by Khrushchev, and it did not have much effect, until almost forty years later.

Until the twentieth century, the Crimean Peninsula was considered part of the Russian Empire. Russia fought a short and bitter war, called the Crimean War (1853-1856), against an alliance of Britain, France, the Ottoman Empire and other countries. *The Charge of the Light Brigade*, made famous by Alfred Lord Tennyson, took place at the Battle of Balaclava and this poem was partially responsible for Britain's desire to end it. The war was marked by many casualties being caused by disease, and modern nursing was developed by an English nurse, Florence Nightingale. Just as the American Civil War saw major developments in weapons, so the Crimean War became the "laboratory" for such weapons as explosive shells, railways and the telegraph. The modern British Army came out of the war with the abolishment of buying and selling commissions. The war ended with the 1856 Treaty of Paris, in which Russia accepted defeat and ceded some lands.

227

RICHARD OSBORN

Timeline of Events in the Ukraine Crisis

DATES	EVENTS
30 December 1922	Ukrainian SSR became a founding member of the Soviet Union
24 August 1991	Ukraine declared its independence from Russia after the failed USSR military coup
7 May 2000	Vladimir Putin became President of Russia after Yeltsin resigned
November 2004	Viktor Yushchenko and Yulia Tymoshenko led the Orange Revolution
8 August2008	Russia invaded Georgia to help South Ossetia and Abkhazia break away from Georgia
25 February 2010	Victor Yanukovych became President of Ukraine after defeating Yulia Tymoshenko
29 November 2013	Yanukovych rejected a pending association agreement with the European Union
22 February 2014	President Yanukovych vanished and ultimately turned up in Russia
27 February 2014	Pro-Russian gunmen seized key buildings in the Crimean capital of Sevastopol
17 March 2014	Crimean Parliament declared independence and asked to join the Russian Federation
18 March 2014	Putin signed the bill to absorb Crimea into the Russian Federation
19 March 2014	Russian soldiers stormed Ukrainian Crimea military bases and forced the troops to leave
22 April 2014	Ukraine's acting president ordered new military attacks against eastern separatists
25 May 2014	Petro Poroshenko was elected President of Ukraine but few eastern Ukrainians voted
27 June 2014	European Union signed association agreement with Ukraine
17 July 2014	MH17 flight Amsterdam to Kuala Lumpur was shot down by pro-Russians killing 298
30 July 2014	The EU and U.S. announced new sanctions on Russia for their support of separatists
5 September 2014	Ukraine and the pro-Russian separatists signed a truce agreement in Minsk
3 November 2014	Separatists in the East elected new leaders in polls backed by the Russian Federation
24 November 2014	President Poroshenko announced he would hold referendum to join NATO at future date

On the 26th of April 1986, a Soviet designed nuclear power station at Chernobyl, in northern Ukraine, developed a major problem and exploded, releasing radiation into the air. The radioactive plume travelled with the current winds, and it spread over mainly northern Europe, including Sweden, Finland and Norway. Many Russians and Ukrainians died from radiation poisoning, especially those that helped fight the fire and seal the station with concrete. The entire town was immediately evacuated, and it will probably be deserted for at least fifty years. A twenty mile exclusion zone was set up around the site, and no unauthorized person is allowed to enter it.

The Ukraine declared its independence from the USSR on the 24th of August 1991, and the Soviet Union officially dissolved itself four months later, on the 26th of December. Thirteen out of the fifteen other Soviet Socialist Republics also declared their independence, leaving only Russia and two republics in a federation.

This dissolution of the USSR, and the declaration of an independent Ukraine, caused a major headache for Russia. The Russians had a large naval base in the Crimea that served as an outlet to the Black Sea, and then into the Mediterranean Sea. Russia signed an agreement with the Ukraine that allowed them to use the Crimea naval base. However, this would set up the issue that Putin exploited approximately twenty-three years later.

As the Ukraine declared its independence, besides inheriting the Crimea, it also inherited the world's third-largest nuclear weapons stockpile. The Ukraine had basically a choice, whereby they could use the weapons to deter any would be aggressor, or they could give them up, under certain conditions. They decided to give them up, if they could get the major powers to guarantee that their borders would be respected. On the 5th of December 1994, the United States (President Clinton), United Kingdom (Prime Minister Blair) and Russia (President Yeltsin) signed, what was called, the Budapest Memorandum on Security Assurances. All sides pledged to respect Ukraine's borders, provide assistance if invaded, and refrain from using military force or economic force, to limit Ukraine's sovereignty. In a separate document, China and France gave assurances to also respect Ukraine's sovereignty.

The following are the six points in the Budapest Memorandum, to which each country agreed.

1. Respect Ukrainian independence and sovereignty within its existing borders.
2. Refrain from the threat or use of force against Ukraine.
3. Refrain from using economic pressure on Ukraine in order to influence its politics.
4. Seek immediate United Nations Security Council action to provide assistance to Ukraine, "if Ukraine should become a victim of an act of aggression or an object of a threat of aggression in which nuclear weapons are used".
5. Refrain from the use of nuclear arms against Ukraine.

6. Consult with one another if questions arise regarding these commitments.

In return, the Ukraine agreed to adhere to the Nuclear Test Ban Treaties. Obviously, Vladimir Putin has violated sections one, two three and four of the memorandum, and the other powers, which agreed to the Memorandum, have done nothing. It was just like the piece of paper signed in Munich, back in 1938, by Hitler, Chamberlain, Mussolini and Daladier.

In 1994, Leonid Kuchma was elected President of Ukraine for a five year term, replacing President Leonid Kravchuk, and he was sworn in on the 19th of July 1994. His first term went fairly well, but it was marred by general financial problems, and the International Monetary Fund (IMF) was not too helpful. On the 28th of June 1996, a new constitution was adopted, and in the same year, a new currency was introduced.

Ukraine and Russia initiated a new Friendship Treaty, which amongst other points, allowed Russia to use the Crimean base, for its Black Sea fleet. Both Boris Yeltsin of Russia and Leonid Kuchma signed the treaty, on the 31st of May 1997.

In 1999, there was an accident that cast a shadow on the Kuchma presidency. On the 25th of March of that year, Vyacheslav Chornovil, a nationalist and anti-communist, was killed in a car crash, along with a long time companion and staff member. There were rumors that it was a political murder and not an accident. No proof was ever offered to support the murder conspiracy, although Chornovil had spoken out against President Kuchma.

In October 2001, the Ukraine military shot down a Russian passenger aircraft over the Black Sea, killing all passengers. It was classified as an accident, and the Ukrainian Defense Minister resigned. The next year, President Kuchma got in trouble with the United States and other Western Powers, when he sold an aircraft, early warning system to Iraq. This action was in violation of the 1990 United Nations arms embargo, on Iraq and Saddam Hussein.

President Kuchma's second term, which ended on the 23rd of January 2005, was marred with corruption and embezzlement charges, against his government and certain officials. In the last year of his office, the Orange Revolution took place with Viktor Yushchenko and Yulia Tymoshenko leading it. In 2005, Viktor Yushchenko became the President at the end of Kuchma's second term, and Yulia Tymoshenko became the Prime Minister.

By now, Putin of Russia had been President for five years, and he was becoming a virtual dictator. By controlling the supply of the Russian natural gas that flowed through a pipeline, to the Ukraine and Western Europe, he started to create problems for the Ukrainian government. Moscow briefly cut the gas supply, stating it was for non-payment, while the Ukraine claimed it was political. This was the start of Russia's meddling in the internal affairs of the country.

In March 2008, Russia agreed to a new contract for the gas supply, and tensions between the two countries seemed to subside. However, the situation only lasted about six months, and then the financial crisis in the West caused major economic problems for the Ukraine. In January 2009, Moscow again halted the delivery of gas supplies for non-payment, and this caused a shortage of natural gas, not only in the Ukraine, but also in Europe. After the Europeans applied considerable pressure on the Ukraine and Russia, a new ten year agreement was finally signed, for the supply of gas,

In February 2010, President Yanukovych won a second term in office, after charges of election fraud were dismissed. Soon thereafter, Yulia Tymoshenko resigned as Prime Minister and was replaced by Mykola Azarov, an ally of the president. On the 21st of April, the Ukraine Parliament ratified a treaty extending the lease of the Crimean naval base to Russia, for another twenty-five years. Just about forty-five days later, on the 3rd of June 2010, the Ukrainian Parliament voted to abandon any request to join NATO.

The year 2011 saw several criminal cases that affected current and former political figures. In many cases, it appeared that politics was more important than the evidence in the cases. Yulia Tymoshenko was put on trial for corruption, misuse of state funds and abuse of power, while she was the Prime Minister. In addition, her Interior Minister was also charged with mishandling state funds. In March of 2011, the former President Kuchma was accused of killing a journalist, Georiy Gongadze, in the year 2000. He denied taking part in the murder. On the 11th of October 2011, the former Prime Minister Tymoshenko was found guilty and sentenced to prison, over her abuse of power in a gas deal with Russia in 2009. As a result, the European Union warned the Ukraine that there would be profound consequences, for this political witch hunt.

In July of 2012, the European Court of Human Rights condemned the detention of a former interior minister on trumped up charges. During the year, some protests took place, mainly in the capital of Kiev, against the government and a new law, which allowed the use of the Russian language, in certain regions of the country.

In April 2013, the European Court of Human Rights again criticized the Ukraine, condemning the arrest and incarceration of the former Prime Minister Yulia Tymoshenko, stating it was unlawful. In July, Russia applied economic pressure on the Ukraine, by halting imports of chocolate, from a major Ukrainian company. Russia was accused of placing an embargo on Ukrainian chocolate, in order to force the government to cancel any plans for joining the EU.

On the 21st of November 2013, the Ukrainian government decided to abandon plans to initial an agreement, with the European Union, that would provide quasi membership. Protesters took to the streets of Kiev, accusing the government of trying to placate Russia. A month later, Russia reduced the price of their natural gas and purchased some Ukrainian debt, in an attempt to mollify the Ukrainians.

Thus began the fateful year of 2014 for the Ukraine. As the year opened, anti-government protesters flooded the streets, and in turn, the government security forces started a major crack down on the rioters. In the middle of January, Parliament passed some new anti-protest laws, as the protesters stormed government offices and the death toll started to rise. More protesters crowded Independence Square in downtown Kiev, and Parliament annulled the new anti-protest laws they had passed just a week before.

In February, the protests became larger, and the clashes with security forces were more frequent. By the middle of February 2014, it was estimated that up to one hundred protesters had been killed and over five hundred wounded. In addition, at least three policemen were killed.

On the 21st of February 2014, President Yanukovych fled the capital of Kiev, and in a few days, took refuge in Russia. He never returned to the Ukraine. The opposition took control of Kiev and installed an interim new president and prime minister, until elections could take place. Russia refused to recognize the new government. Soon, reports started coming out of the Ukraine, about how Yanukovych had plundered the national treasury, and misused government money, to live in a lavish lifestyle.

On the 27th of February, some troops, claiming to be Ukrainian separatists, seized Ukrainian government buildings, in the Crimean Peninsula. All signs pointed to a false flag operation, conducted by the Russian military. While these troops were in possession of the regional parliament building, Russian flags were raised and barricades were erected. The Crimean Council of Ministers was dissolved, and a new Prime Minister was designated to run the region. Security checkpoints were set up throughout the whole region, and soon Crimea was cut off from the Ukraine. In the matter of two days, Ukraine had no control on what happened in the Crimea.

On the 1st of March 2014, the new Crimea authorities took over Ukrainian military facilities and controlled the exits from them. Vladimir Putin sent Russian troops into the Crimean region to assist the separatists, after receiving authorization from the Federation Council of Russia. By the next day, Russian troops moved heavy equipment into Crimea, and they took over the naval base at Sevastopol. The ultimate goal was to seize control of the entire peninsula, in total disregard for the 1994 Budapest Memorandum that Russia had signed. Putin wanted the Crimea Peninsula to become part of Russia again.

Kashin class destroyer in Sevastopol Harbor

"Smetlivyy2007Sevastopol" by Водник.

On the 16th of March, a referendum was held in Crimea, and 97% of the people voted to join the Russian Federation. The result was a foregone conclusion, since the separatists and the Russians controlled the balloting. On the 18th of March, Putin signed a bill approving the integration of Crimea into

Russia, and Russia officially annexed the Crimea on the same day. The Russians and the separatists seized Ukrainian military bases and effectively shut them down, forcing the soldiers to return to the Ukraine. Since Putin violated the Budapest Memorandum agreement, which the Russian Federation and the West had signed in 1994, the West imposed economic sanctions on Russia. However, so far, these sanctions have not had much effect in controlling the actions of Russia in the Ukraine. The price of oil has probably damaged the Russian economy, more than the sanctions have.

More will be written about all of this in the Situation Analysis at the end of this chapter.

On the 17th of April 2014, President Putin publicly acknowledged that the Russian military had backed the Ukrainian separatists, in order to protect the rights of Ukrainian Russians (just like Hitler in the Sudetenland in 1938). He also stated that the Crimean people wanted to join Russia of their own free will, as shown in the referendum a month earlier. Ukraine argued that Russia had violated the agreements, between Ukraine and Russia, concerning the naval base in Sevastopol and also the 1994 Memorandum. Of course, this was to no avail, and the West was not willing to do much about it, except to place economic sanctions on Russia.

For the rest of 2014 and the beginning of 2015, Russia began using Hitler's playbook again, just as they did for the Crimea and the two regions in Georgia a few years earlier. Russia needs a solid land "bridge" to the Crimea from Russia, so for the last nine months, the Russians have been fomenting trouble in the Donetsk and Luhansk Oblasts of the Ukraine. Both regions contain many people of Russian descent, and they are ripe for Putin to try and take away from the Ukraine. In addition, he would obtain the land bridge that is needed to service the Crimea region, without going through the Ukraine. From the beginning of May 2014 to now, there has been considerable fighting in these two regions, between Ukrainian troops and Russian separatists, supported by the regular Russian military.

On the 26th of May, the first battle for Donetsk International Airport took place, with the Ukraine government forces winning the first round.

On the 17th of July 2014, Malaysia Airlines Flight MH17 was destroyed by a Russian built BUK SA-17 anti-aircraft missile system, provided to the separatists by the Russians. All 298 passengers and crew were killed, as the plane disintegrated and fell out of the sky, from over an altitude of 30,000 feet. It was travelling from Amsterdam to Kuala Lumpur and was passing over the Ukraine, when it was shot down. In the same month, on the 23rd, the International Red Cross issued a statement claiming that there was a civil war raging throughout the Ukraine..

Many refugees traveled either to Russia, or the western part of the Ukraine, in order to escape the fighting, mainly in the Donetsk and Luhansk Oblasts (provinces). On the 12th of August, Russia sent a convoy of trucks, ostensibly filled with humanitarian aid, to the Ukraine, and it crossed the border, without permission from the Ukrainian government officials.

The trucks were painted white to indicate the fact that they did not carry munitions or weapons. Since the convoy was not inspected, there was no certainty as to what was carried in the vehicles.

On the 5th of September 2014, there was a meeting between the Ukrainian government and the separatists in Minsk, Belarus. An agreement was signed to initiate a ceasefire and hold elections in the two separatist Oblasts of Donetsk and Luhansk, under Ukrainian law on the 7th of December. The ceasefire was repeatedly violated, by both sides, and the civil war continued on.

The second battle for the Donetsk airport started on the 28th of September, in violation of the ceasefire signed in Minsk. This time the fighting continued for three to four months, and it was intense on both sides. Finally, the separatists captured it, on the 21st of January 2015, and the government forces withdrew. It was a hollow victory however, as the airport runways and buildings were essentially destroyed.

The Russian separatists "jumped the gun", and they held elections on the 2nd of November in both the Donetsk and Luhansk People's Republics, also known as the Donbass region. The elections were held to select chief executives and parliaments, for both of the regions. This was in violation of the Minsk agreement. The West and the Ukraine declared the elections were invalid, and not legitimate, while Russia stated they were an important step in the two contested regions.

Russia still needed that "land bridge" to connect Crimea to the Russian mainland. To those ends, there has been considerable fighting in and around Mariupol, which is a major city on the road, down the Ukrainian coast, to the Crimean Oblast. Russian separatists, supported by Russian military, are trying to carve out a route, until a bridge can be built to bypass the Ukraine. This civil war will probably continue until either Russia controls the Ukraine totally or neutralizes the western part, so it doesn't join NATO or the EU.

In January 2015, a Russian company was awarded a contract to build a twelve mile bridge across the Kerch Straits, which would provide a direct link between Russia and the Crimea. Basically it would link the Russian highway M25 to the Crimean highway M17. This bridge was actually an old idea first dreamed up by Albert Speer, of the German Nazi government, in 1943. It was never built, but in 2010 an agreement was signed, between the Ukraine and Russia, for its construction. However, construction of the bridge was never started. The current contract, to a Russian company, calls for it to be completed by the year 2018.

As the year 2015 continues, the civil war in the Ukraine can be expected to persist for some time to come. Lately, the cities of Kramatorsk and Debal'tseve, in the Donetsk Oblast, have come under attack by separatists. Sixty-seven percent of the people in Kramatorsk speak Russian and twenty-seven percent are ethnic Russians. In Debal'tseve, which is a major railway hub between Donetsk and Luhansk, about thirty-three percent are ethnic Russians.

A new ceasefire was agreed to at a meeting in Minsk, Belarus on the 15th of February 2015, but already there have been violations of the agreement.

*Note: The April 2011 edition of the **National Geographic** (pages 62-81) has an excellent article on the Crimea titled "A Jewel in Two Crowns".*

Situation Analysis:

On the 25th of April 2005, in his annual state of the nation address to the Russian parliament, Putin called the breakup of the Soviet Union, the greatest geopolitical tragedy of the 20th century. The events in Georgia in August 2008, and the lack of support by the West, fueled Putin's desire to put the USSR back together. As noted in a previous chapter, this indecisiveness, by the West, was **APPEASEMENT** and Putin took notice. He started to set his sights on his next victim; the Ukraine.

Three Oblasts in the Ukraine contain a high percentage of ethnic Russians; Crimea 58.3%, Donetsk 38.2% and Luhansk 39.0%. For comparison, according to the 1921 census, taken in Czechoslovakia, an estimated 32.6% of Bohemians were German speaking and 20.5% of Moravians spoke German. Most of the German speaking Czechs were located in the border areas of the two provinces mentioned. These border areas, as noted in a previous chapter, were called the Sudetenland.

Thus, Putin had an almost direct comparison for the three Oblasts in the Ukraine, with "Hitler's" Sudetenland. Using the Hitler "playbook" of creating a crisis over nationalistic fervor, Putin played the Ukrainian ethnic Russians against the more western part of the Ukraine. He made the issue of trying to protect the abused and discriminated ethnic Russians, as the reason for helping the Ukrainian separatists in their fight against the central government in Kiev.

The Crimea, besides having the largest ethnic Russians in the Ukraine, contained an important naval base for Russia. It gave them access to the warm Black Sea that was never blocked by ice. This was critical, since it gave the Russians easy access to the Mediterranean Sea. One argument used by the Russians was that the Crimea was always Russian, until 1954, when Khrushchev gave it to the Ukraine as a goodwill gesture. The former Soviet leader never foresaw the breakup of the USSR.

The West, consisting of the United States, Britain and France, had signed agreements with Russia in 1994, guaranteeing the borders of the Ukraine, in return for them giving up their nuclear weapons. When Russia invaded the Ukraine and took control of the Crimean Peninsula, the West did not do anything, in support of the Ukraine, except impose sanctions on some Russian citizens and organizations. No military aid or action was forthcoming from the Obama administration or the EU. This inaction, by the Obama administration and the other signatories of the Budapest Memorandum, amounted to **APPEASEMENT**. President Putin must have noticed this lack of response by the West, and it encouraged him to go after the next two Oblasts; Donetsk and Luhansk.

It should be noted here that economic sanctions very rarely work, since it is difficult to get all countries to go along with them. In the 1930's FDR placed sanctions on Japan, in response to their invasion of

China and Manchuria. These sanctions included a ban on the export of oil, scrap metal and other commodities to Japan. This made Japan desperate, since they only had enough oil to last a little over a year. Instead of forcing them to withdraw from the Asian mainland, they planned a sneak attack on the United States in the Pacific, thus forcing the Americans back to the U.S. mainland. The point is that the sanctions actually created the opposite effect, as was anticipated.

Economic sanctions have not had much of an effect on Putin since some countries, like China, will still trade with them. The sanctions may actually create a more dangerous Putin, who will take risks. He will continue to destabilize the Ukraine and create friendly governments, with their Russian speaking citizens, in the Donetsk and Luhansk Oblasts. Since the Obama administration, and the West, has no desire to stand up militarily to the Russian dictator, they will continue to APPEASE Putin, while he accomplishes his goals in the Ukraine. Putin wants either the Ukraine to collapse or at least not become part of NATO or the European Union.

Most of the European countries in NATO have drastically reduced their armed forces over the past twenty years, in order to pay for their socialist programs. An example of this hollowing out of armed forces is the United Kingdom. In 1980, Britain had 320,600 full time service personnel, but by the year 2010, the armed forces were reduced to 191,700 personnel. This amounted to a reduction of forty percent, and by 2020, it is planned to be reduced by another twenty percent. America, under the Obama administration, is also hollowing out its armed forces, in a similar fashion.

One can expect that Putin, after gobbling up or neutralizing the Ukraine, will set his sights on either Estonia or Latvia. Both of these countries are in NATO, which will set up a confrontation, between Russia and NATO. Putin wants to determine if NATO exists anymore, and whether it has any teeth.

The population of Estonia consists of 25.2% ethnic Russians and Latvia has 26.0% of its population relating to the Motherland of Russia. Either of these countries will be a tempting target for Putin, if he is not overthrown before then. Currently, eighty one percent of Russians support Putin, even though the ruble has lost value, due to the price of oil and the sanctions.

Putin knows that he has two more years to make his moves, before Barack Obama is out of office and a new president is inaugurated. It will take at least one to two years, or more, for the new United States president to reverse direction and build up the country's economy and military. So, in effect, Russian President Vladimir Putin has three to four years to put the Soviet Union back together, without expecting any interference from the United States or NATO.

Based on President Obama's reaction to events around the world, during the past six years, Vladimir Putin figures that he is dealing with a weak and naïve leader, and he will act accordingly.

22

Conclusion

Originally this chapter was going to analyze the one main blunder or appeasement of the last one hundred years, and list the reason(s) why it was selected. However, as it turned out, I determined there were not one, but two blunders that have had, and will continue to have, a long term effect on the world, and the relationships between countries. The prime criterion for selection was the effect the blunder or appeasement would have on the world over a long period of time. Secondly, was the blunder or appeasement caused by some accidental situation, which was preventable, or was it caused by the person or organization, because they were ignorant or naïve? In the second criteria, the question arises as to whether the responsible party or organization had read history. *See the preface about reading history.*

This chapter will recap the two major blunders and explain why they were and are so important to the Western World, as we know it. I should point out for those readers who notice that not much mention has been made about World War Two, just for the reason that it was not a long war; six years for Europeans and less than four years for Americans. Yes, it was caused by appeasement as outlined in chapter three, but the long term effects, other than the history of the holocaust, turned out to be somewhat short term. Most of the cities that were partially destroyed by bombing have been rebuilt. Of course, it is realized that people, who lost a loved one in the war, will miss them, until they themselves die.

1. VLADIMIR LENIN 1917 – GERMAN BLUNDER

The first blunder was the one that influenced events in the world for over seventy years, and since the beginning of the 21st century, it has become a problem again. Specifically, the special train that Germany provided to Vladimir Lenin to transport him, his wife and his party of about thirty-one supporters through Germany, during the Great War. The decision by the Germans was very short sighted. They wanted Russia out of the war, so Germany could transfer troops from the Eastern front to the Western front. They hoped to give France and Great Britain a knockout blow, before the American troops arrived and entered the war.

Prussian Series P-8
Steam Locomotive

Photo: Bernd Untiedt

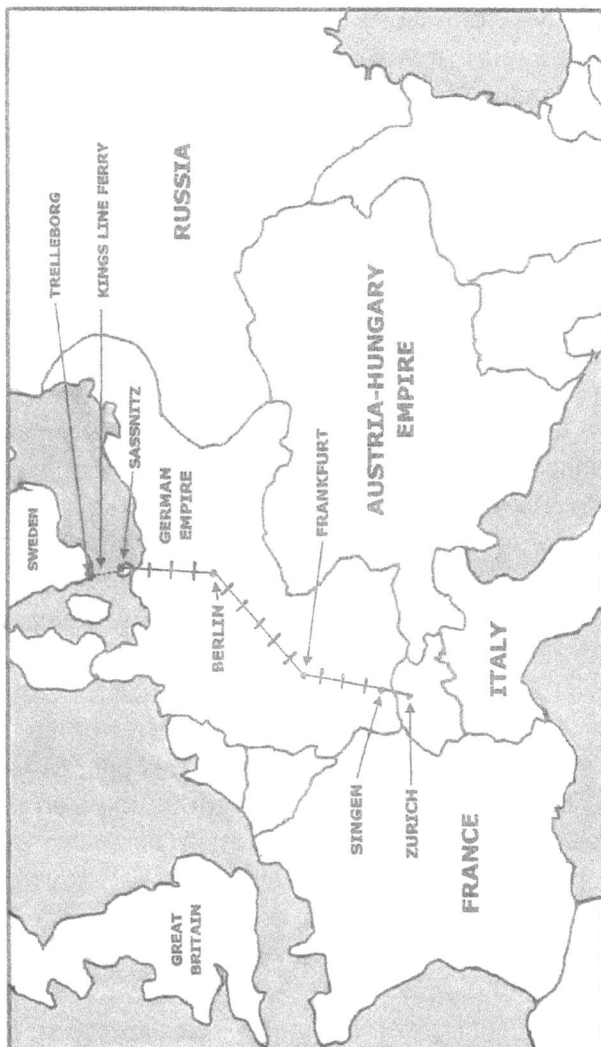

LENIN'S TRAIN RIDE THROUGH GERMANY, APRIL 1917

The decision, to permit the Bolshevik Lenin, and his party, to transit Germany by train from Singen to Sassnitz, was ultimately made by Chancellor Theobald von Bethmann-Hollweg. He had been German Chancellor since the 14th of July 1909, and he resigned on the 13th of July 1917, just three months after Lenin was allowed to travel through Germany. The Chancellor had come under increasing criticism, even before this incident. He never informed Kaiser Wilhelm II of the Lenin issue, and the Kaiser only found out later, what his Chancellor had done. The German General Staff actually approved of the plan, before it went to the Chancellor for his approval.

The German generals knew of Lenin's background and what his philosophy was, but they thought that the advantages far outweighed the disadvantages. They never looked at the possible long term effects, of having a Bolshevik Russia to the east of them. The idea that Lenin might turn against Germany and Europe, never occurred to the German generals, who approved the plan. The German State Secretary, Arthur Zimmermann, who was directly under the Chancellor, was also a key person in this plan to assist Lenin. Besides helping Lenin travel through Germany, the Bolsheviks and their organization were also given funds by the Germans, to help them get started in Russia. The Germans also provided financial aid to help establish the Bolsheviks main propaganda newspaper – Pravda.

Vladimir Lenin, and his party, boarded the train at Singen, about seven miles from the German/Swiss frontier. The one-carriage train, probably pulled by a

Prussian P-8 locomotive, went from Singen to Frankfurt to Berlin and on to Sassnitz, a distance of approximately 770 miles. The carriage, they were in, was sealed, and no Germans were allowed to enter it. At Sassnitz, they left the train and boarded the Kings Line ferry for Trelleborg, Sweden, and then went on to Petrograd.

Once in Russia, Lenin led the Bolshevik revolution that took over the country on the 7th of November 1917 (by the Gregorian calendar) or the 25th of October 1917 (by the Julian calendar) and caused seventy years of hardship for the citizens. After the revolution, the country officially switched from the Julian to the Gregorian calendar. Vladimir Lenin declared a ceasefire on the 15th of December 1917, and he pulled Russia out of the Great War, just as the Germans had hoped. However, it didn't do the Germans much good, because less than one year later, their armies were exhausted, and they had to sue for peace.

The problem, the Germans created, lived on for another seventy years. The communist country of Russia, which later became the Union of Soviet Socialist Republics, was a menace to the Western powers until 1991. Lenin only lived until 1924, and then Joseph Stalin took over, even though Lenin was suspicious of him, before he died. Stalin ruled the Soviet Union with an iron fist, and millions died from famine, murder, execution and other reasons. Stalin conducted many purges of people around him, because he was always concerned they might become more popular than him and gather too much power.

According to estimates, thirty-four to forty-nine million deaths were directly linked to activities caused by Stalin. Many murders were carried out by the NKVD (secret police) on Stalin's orders.

Finally, Stalin died of a stroke in March 1953, but the USSR survived another thirty-eight years under various leaders, until 1991. From 1991 until the early 2000s, the Russian President Boris Yeltsin tried to bring Russia up to the standards of the West, by improving the economy and adopting western capitalist principles.

However, when Vladimir Putin became President of Russia in the year 2000, the relationship between the West and Russia started to change. Putin rode the high price of oil to finance the government, including the military. His overall goal is to put "Humpty Dumpty back together again" or rather the Soviet Union.

His first target was Georgia, the birth place of Joseph Stalin, where there were two provinces that contained ethnic Russians, and both of them had declared independence in 1994, even though they were part of Georgia (chapter thirteen of this book). Putin used the ruse of claiming that he was saving the people of the two provinces from the overly domineering, central government of Georgia.

Then, Putin set his sights on the Ukraine, especially the Crimea. He took the Crimean Peninsula, almost without firing a shot. However, he needed a land bridge to the Crimea from Russia, and that is why the Donetsk and Luhansk Oblasts are the latest targets for Putin. His goal is either to take over the entire country of the Ukraine, or at least neutralize it. In other words, Putin does not want it to become part of NATO or the European Union.

Once Putin has achieved his objectives in the Ukraine, he can be expected to set his sights on at least one of the Baltic States, two have a significant number of ethnic Russians, and/or even the country of Kazakhstan. The leader of Kazakhstan is seventy-four years old, and when he dies, there could be a period of instability that Putin could take advantage of. The ethnic Russians make up today 23.3% of the total country's population of eighteen million. There are over one hundred million Russians under Putin, so he would have strength in numbers. The oil and gas reserves of Kazakhstan would also be attractive to Russia. Hitler's playbook, which Putin seems to be following, called for at least 20% ethic nationals in a country, in order to stir up trouble.

While all this is going on, the West is appeasing Putin, even though sanctions have been placed on Russia. Putin's popularity is still very high (around eighty percent) according to independent polls, since the Russians themselves are very nationalistic.

Putin is also making moves in Egypt, since the Obama administration rebuffed the new President Abdel Fattah el-Sisi, after he overthrew the Muslim Brotherhood President Morsi. In 2014, Egypt and Russia signed an accord, whereby Russia would sell small arms, artillery and anti-aircraft systems to Egypt. It is suspected that Putin is also eyeing a naval base for the Russian fleet, in Egypt. This port would be useful in case his ally, President Assad, is overthrown, with the result that Russia could lose their existing naval base in Syria.

The following section taken from a speech, by Ronald Reagan in October 1964, is as appropriate today, as it was then. This speech was named "Time for Choosing" or "The Speech".

"……………*Admittedly there is a risk in any course we follow other than this, but every lesson in history tells us that the greater risk lies in* **appeasement**, *and this is the specter our well-meaning liberal friends refuse to face--that their policy of accommodation is* **appeasement**, *and it gives no choice between peace and war, only between fight and surrender. If we continue to accommodate, continue to back and retreat, eventually we have to face the final demand-- the ultimatum. And what then? When Nikita Khrushchev has told his people he knows what our answer will be? He has told them that we are retreating under the pressure of the Cold War, and someday when the time comes to deliver the ultimatum, our surrender will be voluntary because by that time we will have weakened from within spiritually, morally, and economically. He believes this because from our side he has heard voices pleading for "peace at any price" or "better Red than dead," or as one commentator put it, he would rather "live on his knees than die on his feet." And therein lies the road to war, because those voices don't speak for the rest of us. You and I know and do not believe that life is so dear and peace so sweet as to be purchased at the price of chains and slavery. If nothing in life is* *worth dying for, when did this begin--just in the face of this enemy? Or should Moses have told the children of Israel to live in slavery under the pharaohs? Should Christ have refused the cross? Should the patriots at Concord Bridge have thrown down their guns and refused to fire the shot heard 'round the world? The martyrs of history were not fools, and our honored dead who gave their lives to stop the advance of the Nazis didn't die in vain. Where, then, is the road to peace? Well, it's a simple answer after all………….."*

The "Lenin" **BLUNDER** by the Germans in 1917 has resonated throughout Europe and around much of the world, for the last ninety-eight years. It may last a lot longer, depending on whether the West rearms and takes on Russia. Of course, one also needs to keep an eye on China!

2. SHAH and IRAN 1979 – AMERICAN BLUNDER

The other main **BLUNDER**, by the West, was in 1979, and the Carter administration was mostly responsible for it. The main people involved in this sordid **BLUNDER** were President Jimmy Carter and Secretary of State Cyrus Vance. Both of these men had very little experience in foreign affairs. President Carter was a Governor of the State of Georgia before becoming President, and Cyrus Vance was a trial lawyer from New York. How Vance managed to get the job as Secretary of State is a major question? Although he was in the Defense Department and also involved in the Vietnam negotiations, he obviously had probably not read very much history.

Regardless, Carter and Vance were responsible for convincing the Shah to leave Iran in 1979, even though neither Carter nor Vance seemed to have any idea of what was going to follow. The United States withdrew support from the Shah in 1978, because he would not follow Carter's and Vance's requests to release political prisoners and other matters. What the Carter administration didn't understand was that, when the Shah departed, it would lead to a major power vacuum in Iran. Ayatollah Khomeini and his followers were ready to fill this void of leadership in Iran, and their method of governing would be a lot worse, than anything the Shah ever did.

Maybe, President Carter, who was and is a religious (Baptist) person, thought that, since Khomeini was also religious, he would be a good leader for Iran, as he, himself, was for the United States. Carter appeared to realize the error of his ways in late 1979 and 1980, but by then, it was too late. The Muslim extremists had taken over Iran and were spreading their hatred of the West, throughout the region and the world.

Since Khomeini and the Mullahs took over Shiite Iran in 1979, they have spread their faith throughout many areas of the world. It is obvious that Iran's goal is to develop the atom bomb, and a missile upon which to mount it. Then, they can threaten their neighbors (Sunni or Shia) and even Europe, with all its infidels. Iran has helped finance and arm Hamas, Hezbollah and other terrorist groups throughout the Middle East and North Africa.

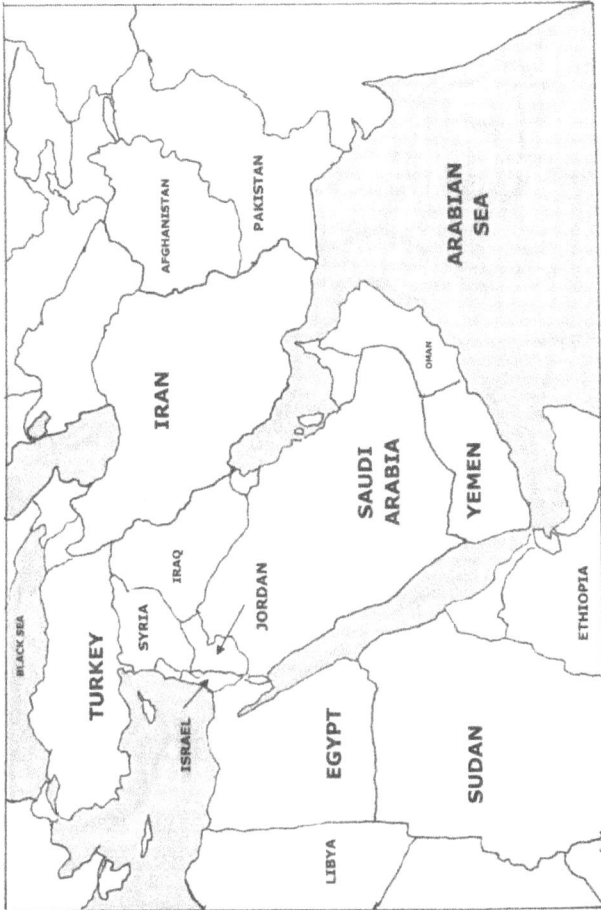

MIDDLE EAST MAP

Even Winston Churchill foresaw the Islamic problems arising from the Middle East and North Africa, when he wrote a speech back in 1899.

"How dreadful are the curses which Mohammedanism lays on its votaries! Besides the fanatical frenzy, which is as dangerous in a man as hydrophobia in a dog, there is this fearful fatalistic apathy.

The effects are apparent in many countries, improvident habits, slovenly systems of agriculture, sluggish methods of commerce, and insecurity of property exist wherever the followers of the Prophet rule or live. A degraded sensualist deprives this life of its grace and refinement, the next of its dignity and sanctity.

The fact that in Mohammedan law every woman must belong to some man as his absolute property, either as a child, a wife, or a concubine, must delay the final extinction of slavery until the faith of Islam has ceased to be a great power among men. Individual Muslims may show splendid qualities, but the influence of the religion paralyses the social development of those who follow it.

No stronger retrograde force exists in the world. Far from being moribund, Mohammedanism is a militant and proselytizing faith. It has already spread throughout Central Africa, raising fearless warriors at every step; and were it not that Christianity is sheltered in the strong arms of science, the science against which it had vainly struggled, the civilization of

modern Europe might fall, as fell the civilization of ancient Rome."
Sir Winston Churchill; (Source: The River War, first edition, Vol II, pages 248-250 London).

Since the United States pulled out of Iraq at the end of 2011, Iran has increasingly worked with the Nouri al-Maliki and Haidar al-Abadi governments, in order to make sure the Sunnis do not take over again in that country. Iran is also helping Bashar Assad to stay in power in Syria, since they want to keep open the conduit for arms supplies to Hezbollah. Most arms, supplied by Iran to Hamas and Hezbollah, go through Syria, and then go on to Lebanon or the Gaza strip.

Just recently, the Shiite Houthis in Yemen took over that country, and Iran is a backer of this Islamic extremist group. It cannot be said that all Islamic extremist groups are controlled by Iran, but you can bet Iran tries to influence them, as much as possible, in their favor. In February 2015, the Houthis signed an air transport agreement with Tehran, whereby there will be twelve weekly flights from Iran to Yemen.

Some of the major groups spreading hatred and violence through the Middle East and Africa today are:

- IS (ISIS, ISIL)
- al-Qaeda
- Boko Haram – Nigeria
- Boko Haram – Cameroon
- al-Nusra – Libya

- Houthis – Yemen
- Taliban – Afghanistan
- Muslim Brotherhood – Egypt
- GIA – Algeria
- Ansar al-Sharia – Tunisia
- al-Shabaab – Chad
- Boko Haram – Chad
- Hamas – Palestine Gaza Strip
- Hezbollah – Lebanon
- LIFG Libyan Islamic Fighting Group

The above is only a partial list, although it does contain some of the major terrorist organizations in existence today. The original organization named al-Qaeda, founded by Osama bin Laden, has now morphed into several different terrorist organizations that only cooperate with each other, when it suits the leaders.

For the past thirty-five years, Iran's shadow has grown ominous, and it is spreading over the entire Middle East. Just recently in Egypt, some terrorists struck the North Sinai capital of el-Arish and the town of Rafah, in a coordinated attack. In addition, an IS group called Ansar Beit al-Maqdis launched several attacks on the Egyptian police and military. They also appear to be followers of the banned Muslim Brotherhood.

The *Western* powers are again negotiating with Tehran over the Iranian nuclear programs, but already there are signs of **APPEASEMENT**. In the last round of negotiations, a **deadline,** of the 1st of March 2015, was set for a political accord and a deadline, of the 1st

July of 2015, for the final agreement. The State Department, on the 9th of February 2015, stated, through Jen Psaki the State Department spokesperson that the March 1st date was not a deadline, but that it was just a goal. This is not the wording in the November accord that set the new dates. They were called deadlines. Obviously, President Obama, Valerie Jarrett and Secretary of State John Kerry are trying to get an agreement, in any way they can. This is called **APPEASEMENT**.

Perhaps, John Kerry has the ultimate objective of receiving the Nobel Peace Prize by signing any nuclear agreement with Iran, regardless of the details (the devil is in the details). President Obama, who received the Nobel Peace Prize in 2009, for nothing, would probably like to justify it with an Iranian/U.S. nuclear pact.

The **BLUNDER** by the Carter administration has resonated all the way through to the present day, and there does not appear to be any end in sight, short of a regime change in Iran. This begs the question as to what is the Obama administration doing about trying to create a regime change in Iran; probably nothing.

In summation, there were two massive blunders in the past century, which we have analyzed in the appropriate chapters previously. They were:

1. **VLADIMIR LENIN 1917 – GERMAN BLUNDER**
2. **SHAH and IRAN 1979 - AMERICAN BLUNDER**

The title of this book, *Twilight for the West?,* was selected by the author because, in his opinion, unless the *Western* politicians wake up, we could be seeing the sunset of the *Western* way of life.

The U.S. and European military budgets have been cut to the bone, mainly to pay for the entitlements the people have been promised and expect. In addition, with the demographics and its increasing number of older people in the advanced countries, it will be difficult, but not impossible, to reverse the trend of decline.

Readers of this book must make up their own minds and act accordingly.

TWILIGHT FOR THE WEST?

AVAILABLE NOW

The Osborns' novel is about a young British lieutenant, Ian Black, who arrives in Cyprus and soon comes face-to-face with EOKA terrorists. He falls in love with a nurse at the hospital and saves the Cyprus Governor from assassination. Ian survives an attempt on his life but to his horror faces a tragedy. He returns to England after helping to save the Cyprus peace treaty.

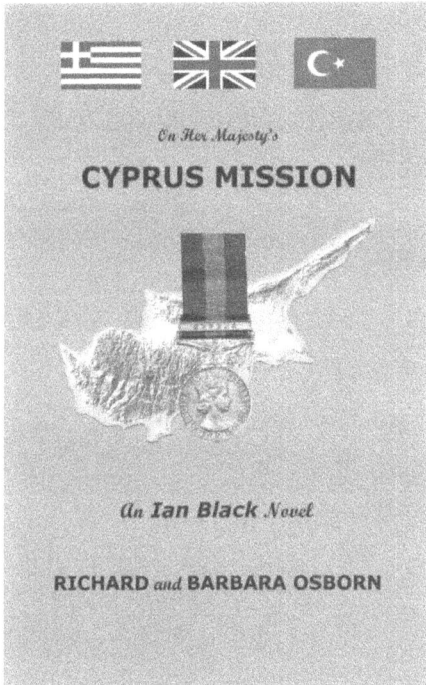

On Her Majesty's

CYPRUS MISSION

An Ian Black Novel

RICHARD and BARBARA OSBORN

BRITANNIA-AMERICAN PUBLISHING
ISBN: 978069229424

RICHARD OSBORN

AVAILABLE NOW

Ian Black is transferred to Berlin after graduating from the
Advanced Intelligence Corps Academy. He arrives just in
time to be involved before and after the construction of the
Wall. He befriends an East German politician's mistress and
assists a Czechoslovakian ice skater in her defection to the
West. Ian follows the Russian troop movements in the East.

On Her Majesty's
BERLIN MISSION

An **Ian Black** *Novel*

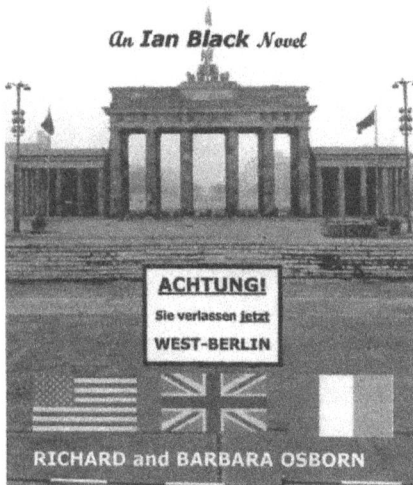

BRITANNIA-AMERICAN PUBLISHING
ISBN: 9780692780855

AVAILABLE NOW

After resigning his commission in the British Army and going to the United States, Ian Black meets with General Carter in Washington. He is offered a commission in the USAF and works in the Air Force ISR Agency as a Captain. Due to his experience in Berlin, he is transferred to the USAFSS Section H during the Vietnam War.

BRITANNIA-AMERICAN BOOKS
ISBN: 9781981773022

RICHARD OSBORN

True Patriotism is a trilogy novel that develops the career of Ian Black, first in the British Army and ultimately the United Sates Air Force. This book is a combination of the novels "On Her Majesty's Cyprus Mission, "On Her Majesty's Berlin Mission" and "On the President's Vietnam Mission". It combines the military action and adventure into 700 pages.

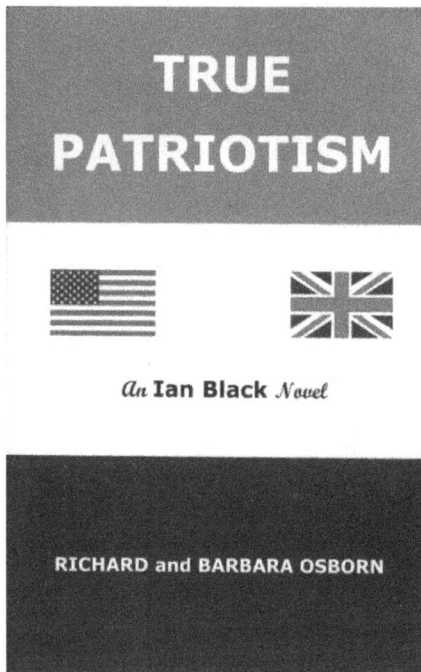

TRUE
PATRIOTISM

An **Ian Black** *Novel*

RICHARD and BARBARA OSBORN

BRITANNIA-AMERICAN BOOKS
ISBN: 9781719086462

AVAILABLE NOW

The Osborns' explosive novel delves into whether the President, Edward Tuckwell, is able to remain in office after two terms, using a false flag operation. The climax shocks the nation and calm finally returns to Washington, after the tanks knock down the White House gates. Although this is a novel, readers have to decide whether something like this could actually happen

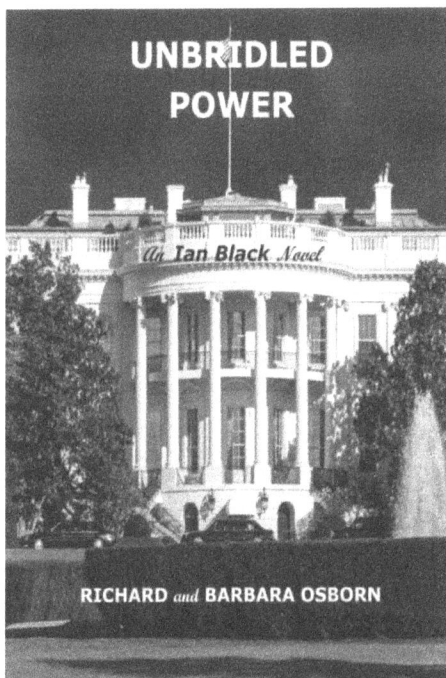

UNBRIDLED POWER

An Ian Black Novel

RICHARD and **BARBARA OSBORN**

BRITANNIA-AMERICAN PUBLISHING
ISBN: 9780692503379

If readers of this book have any comments about the material or the analysis, you are invited to email them to:

BritanniaAmericanPublishing@yahoo.com

www.ingramcontent.com/pod-product-compliance
Lightning Source LLC
LaVergne TN
LVHW011345080426
835511LV00005B/131